Garlic Cookbook

Garlic Recipes Everyone Should Learn

By
BookSumo Press

Published by
http://www.booksumo.com

LEGAL NOTES

Table of Contents

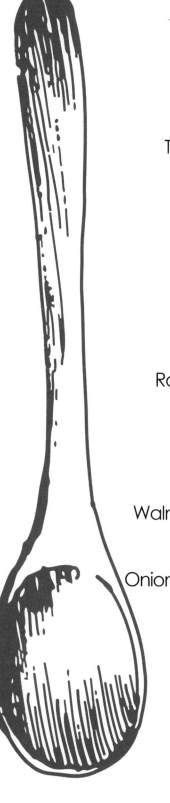

Indonesian Inspired Beef Curry 32

Sweet Potato Ginger Veggie Curry 33

Country Curried Cabbage 34

October's Pumpkin Curried Soup 35

Tofu Curry 101 36

Kerala Fish Curry 37

Jamaican Style Shrimp Curry 38

Alternative Pumpkin Curry 39

Seafood Curry Dinner 40

South Indian Prawn Curry 41

Thai Sardine Curry 42

Rustic Country Squash Pancakes 43

French Bean and Parmesan Casserole 44

Turkey Soup 45

Lentils from Morocco 46

Artisan Style Shiitake Mushrooms and Lentils 47

Rustic Lentils with Savory Chicken 48

Sunbelt Quinoa Classic 49

Lentil Soup 50

Quinoa Festivalt 51

Chipotle Quinoa 52

Squash and Garbanzos Couscous 53

Cherry Tomatoes, Onions, and Basil Couscous 54

Homemade Piri Piri 55

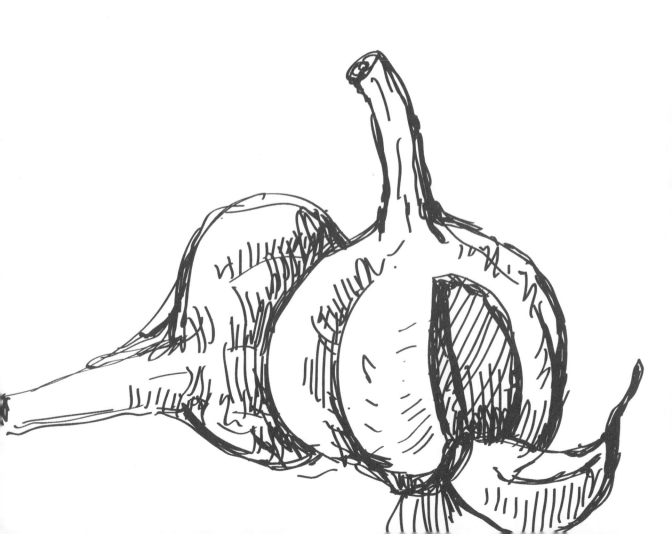

Eggplant
in Japan

🥣 Prep Time: 20 mins
🕐 Total Time: 35 mins

Servings per Recipe: 6
Calories   212 kcal
Fat   10.3 g
Carbohydrates   29.9g
Protein   5 g
Cholesterol   0 mg
Sodium   445 mg

Ingredients

2 tbsps vegetable oil
4 Japanese eggplants, cut into 1-inch cubes
2 tbsps vegetable oil
2 onions, thinly sliced
1 tbsp minced garlic
2 tbsps soy sauce
2 tbsps water

1 1/2 tbsps oyster sauce
1 tbsp chili garlic sauce
1 tsp white sugar
ground black pepper to taste
1/2 tsp Asian (toasted) sesame oil

Directions

1. Get a bowl, mix: black pepper, soy sauce, sugar, water, chili garlic sauce, and oyster sauce.
2. Get 2 tbsps of oil very hot in a wok. Then stir fry your eggplants for 6 mins.
3. Place the eggplants to the side.
4. Add in 2 more tbsps of oil and then your onions and garlic for 1 min.
5. Now pour in your soy sauce mix.
6. Set the heat to low and pour the eggplants into the sauce and onions.
7. Cook the eggplants with a light simmer and low heat until most of the liquid has evaporated (about 6 to 7 mins).
8. Add some sesame oil and cook for 1 more min.
9. Enjoy.

EGGPLANT
in Italy

 Prep Time: 30 mins

Total Time: 1 hr

Servings per Recipe: 6

Calories	389 kcal
Fat	30.6 g
Carbohydrates	14.4g
Protein	14.5 g
Cholesterol	41 mg
Sodium	680 mg

Ingredients

1/2 C. Italian-seasoned bread crumbs
1/4 C. grated Parmesan cheese
1 pinch red pepper flakes, or to taste
1 eggplant - trimmed, peeled, and sliced
1/2-inch thick
1/2 C. olive oil
1 (6 oz.) can tomato paste
1 1/2 (6 oz.) cans water
1/4 tsp dried basil
1/4 tsp dried oregano

1/4 tsp dried parsley
1 clove garlic, crushed
1 tsp brown sugar
sea salt and ground black pepper to taste
1 (8 oz.) package fresh mozzarella cheese,
sliced
3/4 C. grated Parmesan cheese

Directions

1. Coat a casserole dish with nonstick spray or oil and then set your oven to 425 degrees before doing anything else.
2. Get a bowl, combine: pepper flakes, bread crumbs, and parmesan (1/4 C.).
3. Coat your eggplant pieces with olive oil and dip them into the bread crump mix.
4. Layer all your eggplants into the greased casserole dish.
5. Cook everything in the oven for 14 mins and then lower the heat to 375 and remove the dish from the oven.
6. Lightly boil the following in a large pot: basil, oregano, pepper, parsley, salt, brown sugar, garlic, water, and tomato paste.
7. Cover the eggplants with the tomato mixture and then add a final layer of parmesan (3/4 C.) and mozzarella.
8. Cook the contents in the oven for 17 mins.
9. Let the dish sit for 10 mins.
10. Enjoy over pasta.

Baba Ghanoush
(Eggplant in Egypt)

Prep Time: 10 mins
Total Time: 1 hr 10 mins

Servings per Recipe: 6	
Calories	83 kcal
Fat	5.1 g
Carbohydrates	9g
Protein	2.2 g
Cholesterol	0 mg
Sodium	9 mg

Ingredients

1 large eggplant
1 head garlic
1 tbsp refined olive oil
2 tbsps lemon juice
2 tbsps tahini

1 tsp Splenda(R) (optional)
salt and pepper to taste

Directions

1. Set your oven to 375 degrees before doing anything else.
2. Cut some small incisions into your eggplant in 5 different places evenly around the entire vegetable.
3. Cook the eggplant in the oven for 30 mins.
4. Slice off the top part of your garlic and coat it with olive oil before placing it in the oven for 20 mins.
5. Shut the heat.
6. Scoop out the insides of the eggplant and put everything into a colander and let the liquid drain out. This should take about 12 mins.
7. Now separate the garlic cloves from their skin and place to the side.
8. Now add the following to your food processor and pulse until smooth: 3 tbsps of garlic, eggplants, tahini, and lemon juice.
9. If the contents are bitter add some sugar, also add some salt.
10. Enjoy with toasted pita.

THAI STYLE
Squash with Peanut Sauce (Vegan Approved)

Prep Time: 15 mins
Total Time: 46 mins

Servings per Recipe: 4

Calories	235 kcal
Fat	15.9 g
Carbohydrates	17.9 g
Protein	10.3 g
Cholesterol	0 mg
Sodium	834 mg

Ingredients

1/2 small spaghetti squash, halved and seeded
1/3 C. peanut butter
2 tbsps tamari
1/2 tsp agave syrup
1/4 tsp sea salt
1/4 tsp minced fresh ginger
1/4 tsp minced garlic
1/2 lime, juiced
1 dash sriracha hot sauce (optional)

1 C. shredded cabbage
1 C. chopped broccoli
1 small cucumber, cut into matchstick-size pieces
1 carrot, shredded
2 scallions, minced
1 sprig fresh mint, thinly sliced
1/4 C. roasted, salted peanuts

Directions

1. Set your oven to 400 degrees before doing anything else.
2. Lay your squash with the insides facing downwards in a jellyroll pan.
3. Cook the veggies in the oven for 35 mins.
4. Get a bowl, combine: garlic, peanut butter, ginger, tamari, sea salt, and agave syrup.
5. Stir the mix a bit then heat everything in the microwave for 60 secs with a high level of heat.
6. Stir the mix then add in the sriracha and lime juice.
7. Get a bowl then scoop the flesh of your squash into it.
8. Combine the following with the squash: mint, cabbage, scallions, broccoli, carrots, and cucumbers.
9. Stir the mix then top everything with your agave sauce and peanuts.
10. Enjoy.

Moroccan Style
Squash

🥣 Prep Time: 45 mins
🕐 Total Time: 2 hrs 45 mins

Servings per Recipe: 6	
Calories	430 kcal
Fat	28.9 g
Carbohydrates	20.9g
Protein	23.7 g
Cholesterol	101 mg
Sodium	1235 mg

Ingredients

1 (2 lb) spaghetti squash, halved and seeded
1 tbsp olive oil
1 lb ground lamb
1 tbsp olive oil
1/2 small chopped red onion
2 red bell peppers, seeded and diced
5 cloves garlic, chopped

1 tbsp dried basil
1 tbsp chopped fresh rosemary
1 tsp dried oregano
salt and pepper to taste
12 oz. ricotta salata cheese, crumbled
12 pimento-stuffed green olives, sliced
1 (15 oz.) can tomato sauce

Directions

1. Cover a jellyroll pan with foil then set your oven to 375 degrees before doing anything else.
2. Perforate the skin of your squash with a fork then place the veggies in the jellyroll pan with the flesh facing downwards.
3. Cook everything in the oven for 65 mins then flip the veggies and let them lose their heat.
4. Begin to stir fry your lamb in 1 tbsp of olive oil for 9 mins then place the meat to the side.
5. Add in 1 more tbsp of oil and begin to stir fry your bell pepper and onions for 7 mins then add in the oregano, garlic, rosemary, and basil.
6. Stir the mix then add in some pepper and salt. Let the mix cook for 4 mins.
7. Now scoop out the insides of your squash into a bowl then add some pepper and salt.
8. Layer 1/2 of the veggies into a casserole dish then layer half of the following on top of them: lamb, tomato sauce, red pepper mix, cheese, and olives.
9. Do this again with the rest of the ingredients starting with the squash.
10. Cook everything in the oven for 35 mins. Enjoy.

SQUASH
and Chicken Stir Fry Stew

🥣 Prep Time: 45 mins
🕐 Total Time: 1 hr 45 mins

Servings per Recipe: 6
Calories	251 kcal
Fat	11.5 g
Carbohydrates	25.5g
Protein	15.1 g
Cholesterol	39 mg
Sodium	561 mg

Ingredients

1 (3 lb) spaghetti squash
2 tbsps olive oil
1 onion, thinly sliced
2 cloves garlic, minced
1 green bell pepper, diced
2 tbsps paprika
1 tsp salt
1 tsp caraway seeds
ground black pepper to taste

3 skinless, boneless chicken breast halves
1 (14.5 ounce) can whole peeled tomatoes, drained
1/2 cup sour cream

Directions

1. Set your oven to 350 degrees before doing anything else.
2. Perforate your squash with a toothpick or fork then place it on a jellyroll pan. Cook the squash in the oven for 50 mins then flip it and continue baking the squash for 12 more mins.
3. Now begin to stir fry the following, in olive oil: black pepper, onions, caraway seeds, garlic, salt, bell peppers, and paprika. Let everything fry for 7 mins.
4. Lower the heat to medium then add in the chicken. Fry the chicken for 11 mins each side until it is fully done. Then place the meat to the side, slice it, and add it back to the pan.
5. Combine in the tomatoes and get everything boiling. Once the mix is boiling, set the heat to low, and let the mix gently cook.
6. Cut your squash into 2 pieces then scrape out the insides into the simmering sauce. Set the heat to its lowest level and let everything cook for 12 mins then add in the sour cream and stir the mix.
7. Enjoy.

Rustic
Cauliflower

Prep Time: 10 mins
Total Time: 40 mins

Servings per Recipe: 4
Calories	176 kcal
Fat	13.8 g
Carbohydrates	12.1g
Protein	4.3 g
Cholesterol	0 mg
Sodium	64 mg

Ingredients

1 large head cauliflower, sliced lengthwise
through the core into 4 'steaks'
1/4 C. olive oil
1 tbsp fresh lemon juice
2 cloves garlic, minced

1 pinch red pepper flakes, or to taste
salt and ground black pepper to taste

Directions

1. Set your oven to 400 degrees before doing anything else.
2. Combine in a bowl: black pepper, olive oil, salt, lemon juice, pepper flakes, and garlic.
3. Layer your cauliflower in a casserole dish evenly.
4. Coat the veggies with half of the wet mix and cook everything in the oven for 17 mins.
5. Flip the veggies and coat them with the remaining mixture.
6. Continue cooking everything for 14 more mins.
7. Enjoy.

STUFFED
Bell Peppers
Italian Style

Prep Time: 10 mins
Total Time: 1 hr 5 mins

Servings per Recipe: 4
Calories	400.5
Fat	19.8g
Cholesterol	124.7mg
Sodium	1294.7mg
Carbohydrates	28.4g
Protein	27.8g

Ingredients

6 green bell peppers
Beef Mixture:
1 lb. ground beef
1/2 C. onion, chopped
1 tbsp garlic, minced
1 egg, whisked
1/2 C. breadcrumbs
1 tbsp parmesan cheese
1 tsp salt
1 tsp ground pepper
1 tsp red pepper flakes (optional)
1/2 tsp oregano
1/4 tsp parsley
Quick Tomato Sauce Topping:
1 C. tomato sauce
1/4 C. water
1 tbsp brown sugar
1 tbsp vinegar
1 tsp prepared mustard
1 tsp Worcestershire sauce
1/4 tsp dried oregano
1/4 tsp dried basil
1/4 tsp garlic powder
1/4 tsp parsley flakes
1/4 tsp salt
1/4 tsp pepper

Directions

1. Set your oven to 350 degrees F before doing anything else and lightly grease a baking dish.
2. Cut off the tops of the bell peppers and discard the seeds from the inside.
3. In a pan of boiling water, blanch the bell peppers for about 5 minutes.
4. In a large bowl, add all the beef mixture ingredients and mix till well combined.
5. In another bowl, mix together all the tomato sauce ingredients.
6. In the bottom of the prepared baking dish, spread about 2 tbsp of the tomato sauce evenly.
7. Stuff each bell pepper with the beef mixture evenly and top with the remaining tomato sauce.
8. Place the vegetables over the tomato sauce in a single layer and cook everything in the oven for about 50-60 minutes.

Anchovies, Kale, and Capers

Prep Time: 25 mins
Total Time: 40 mins

Servings per Recipe: 4	
Calories	361 kcal
Fat	15.6 g
Carbohydrates	41.3g
Protein	15.4 g
Cholesterol	18 mg
Sodium	361 kcal

Ingredients

1/2 (16 oz.) package whole-wheat angel hair pasta
2 tbsps olive oil
1/2 large onion, sliced
2 cloves garlic, minced
1 tsp red pepper flakes
1 tbsp drained capers
1 (2 oz.) can anchovy fillets, drained and quartered
1 C. canned diced tomatoes, undrained
2 C. coarsely chopped kale
1 (4 oz.) can sliced black olives, drained
1/2 C. grated Parmesan cheese, or to taste

Directions

1. Boil your pasta in salt and water for 9 mins. The remove all the liquids.
2. Simultaneously stir fry your garlic, red pepper flakes, and onions for 7 mins in olive oil.
3. Add in: tomatoes, capers, and anchovy.
4. Get this mixture boiling and then add the kale.
5. Lower the heat on the stove and let the kale cook for 12 mins.
6. Add your pasta to the kale mix and also some olives. Garnish the entire dish with parmesan.
7. Enjoy.

ASIAN STYLE
Broccoli with Beef I

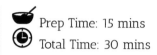

Prep Time: 15 mins

Total Time: 30 mins

Servings per Recipe: 4

Calories	178 kcal
Fat	3.2 g
Carbohydrates	19 g
Protein	19.2 g
Cholesterol	39 mg
Sodium	755 mg

Ingredients

1/4 C. all-purpose flour
1 (10.5 oz.) can beef broth
2 tbsps white sugar
2 tbsps soy sauce
1 lb boneless round steak, cut into bite size pieces

1/4 tsp chopped fresh ginger root
1 clove garlic, minced
4 C. chopped fresh broccoli cheese

Directions

1. Get a bowl, combine until smooth: soy sauce, flour, sugar, and broth.
2. Now stir fry your beef for 5 mins and add the soy sauce mix, broccoli, garlic, and ginger. Get the contents simmering with a high heat and then lower it.
3. Let the soy sauce mix get thick while lightly boiling for about 7 to 12 mins.
4. Enjoy with jasmine rice.

Romano, Basil, Chicken, Caesar Panini

🥄 Prep Time: 20 mins
🕐 Total Time: 36 mins

Servings per Recipe: 2	
Calories	587 kcal
Carbohydrates	20 g
Cholesterol	85 mg
Fat	41.5 g
Protein	32.5 g
Sodium	523 mg

Ingredients

1/4 C. packed fresh basil leaves
1/4 C. olive oil
4 cloves garlic, diced
2 tbsps grated Romano cheese
1 tsp dried oregano
1 tsp ground black pepper
2 skinless, boneless chicken breast halves
2 tbsps creamy Caesar salad dressing
6 slices Italian bread with sesame seeds (Scali)
1/2 C. shredded iceberg lettuce
2 thin slices smoked mozzarella

Directions

1. Heat up your grill and put some oil on the grate
2. Blend a mixture of basil, oregano, oil, garlic, Romano cheese and pepper in a blender until smooth.
3. Now grill chicken on the preheated grill for about 5 minutes each side.
4. Spread Caesar dressing over the bread and put lettuce before putting additional slice of bread over it.
5. Now put cooked chicken breast and smoked mozzarella before closing it up to make a sandwich.
6. Cook this Panini in the preheated grill for about three minutes or until the outside is golden brown.

TARRAGON
Wild Rice Salad

Prep Time: 25 mins
Total Time: 5 hrs 15 mins

Servings per Recipe: 10

Calories	326 kcal
Fat	20.7 g
Carbohydrates	19.2g
Protein	15.9 g
Cholesterol	32 mg
Sodium	390 mg

Ingredients

1 1/2 C. uncooked wild rice
6 C. water
1/3 C. tarragon vinegar
3 tbsps Dijon mustard
1 tbsp white sugar
1 tsp salt
1 clove garlic, minced
1 tsp dried tarragon, crumbled
1/2 tsp black pepper
1/2 tsp crushed red pepper flakes

2/3 C. safflower oil
3 C. cubed cooked chicken
1 C. sliced celery
1/2 C. diced fresh parsley
1/2 C. sliced green onion
1/2 lb sugar snap peas, strings removed
1/2 C. toasted slivered almonds

Directions

1. Get your rice boiling in water, place a lid on the pot, set the heat to low, and let the rice cook for 35 mins.
2. Remove any extra liquids, and stir the rice.
3. Let the rice continue to cook for 7 more mins to remove all the liquids. Then add the rice to a bowl.
4. Get a 2nd bowl, combine: pepper flakes, vinegar, black pepper, mustard, tarragon, sugar, garlic, and salt.
5. Add the safflower oil and whisk the contents until everything is smooth.
6. Now add the following to your rice: green onions, chicken, parsley, and celery.
7. Add in the wet oil mix then stir everything.
8. Place a covering of plastic over the mix and put everything in the fridge for 5 hrs.
9. Now begin to boil your peas in water and salt for 1 min.
10. Remove the liquids and run them under cold water. Once the peas are chilled slice them diagonally.

11. Combine the almonds and the peas with the rice mix and stir the contents evenly then serve the salad.

12. Enjoy.

QUINOA
Pepper Salad

Prep Time: 20 mins
Total Time: 1 hr 30 mins

Servings per Recipe: 12
Calories	148 kcal
Fat	4.5 g
Carbohydrates	22.9g
Protein	4.6 g
Cholesterol	0 mg
Sodium	592 mg

Ingredients

1 tsp canola oil
1 tbsp minced garlic
1/4 C. diced (yellow or purple) onion
2 1/2 C. water
2 tsps salt, or to taste
1/4 tsp ground black pepper
2 C. quinoa
3/4 C. diced fresh tomato
3/4 C. diced carrots
1/2 C. diced yellow bell pepper
1/2 C. diced cucumber

1/2 C. frozen corn kernels, thawed
1/4 C. diced red onion
1 1/2 tbsps diced fresh cilantro
1 tbsp diced fresh mint
1 tsp salt
1/4 tsp ground black pepper
2 tbsps olive oil
3 tbsps balsamic vinegar

Directions

1. Stir fry 1/4 C. of onions and garlic in canola for 7 mins. Then add in: 1/4 tsp black pepper, water, 2 tsps salt.
2. Get everything boiling then add in the quinoa.
3. Place a lid on the pot, set the heat to low, and let the quinoa cook for 22 mins.
4. Remove any excess liquids, place the mix in a bowl, and put everything in the fridge until it is cold, with a covering of plastic.
5. Once the quinoa is cooled combine it with the following: 1/4 tsp black pepper, 1/4 C. red onions, 1 tsp salt, tomato, mint, corn, cilantro, carrots, cucumber, and bell peppers.
6. Top the mix with balsamic and olive oil then stir the contents evenly.
7. Enjoy.

Black Bean and Rice Burgers (Vegetarian Approved)

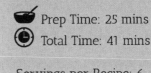 Prep Time: 25 mins

Total Time: 41 mins

Servings per Recipe: 6

Calories	317 kcal
Fat	5.8 g
Carbohydrates	49.4g
Protein	18.2 g
Cholesterol	71 mg
Sodium	1704 mg

Ingredients

1/2 C. uncooked brown rice
1 C. water
2 (16 oz.) cans black beans, rinsed and drained
1 green bell pepper, halved and seeded
1 onion, quartered
1/2 C. sliced mushrooms
6 cloves garlic, peeled

3/4 C. shredded mozzarella cheese
2 eggs
1 tbsp chili powder
1 tbsp ground cumin
1 tbsp garlic salt
1 tsp hot sauce
1/2 C. dry bread crumbs, or as needed

Directions

1. Get your water and rice boiling, then place a lid on the pot, set the heat to low, and let the contents gently cook for 47 mins.
2. Heat up your grill and cover the grate with foil.
3. With a blender, process: garlic, bell pepper, mushrooms, and onions. Then place everything in a bowl.
4. Now blend the mozzarella and the rice and add them to the same bowl
5. Get a 2nd bowl, mash: black beans until paste like.
6. Then add in the blended mix.
7. Get a 3rb bowl, combine: beaten eggs, hot sauce, chili powder, garlic salt, and cumin.
8. Add this to the beans and then mix in your bread crumbs.
9. Shape the bean mix into 6 burgers then grill each for 7 mins per side.
10. Enjoy the patties with sesame seed buns and some mayo.
11. Enjoy.

WALNUTS, BROCCOLI, and Cheddar Brown Rice

 Prep Time: 15 mins
Total Time: 40 mins

Servings per Recipe: 4

Calories	368 kcal
Fat	22.9 g
Carbohydrates	30.4g
Protein	15.1 g
Cholesterol	37 mg
Sodium	643 mg

Ingredients

1/2 C. chopped walnuts
1 tbsp butter
1 onion, chopped
1/2 tsp minced garlic
1 C. uncooked instant brown rice
1 C. vegetable broth
1 lb fresh broccoli florets

1/2 tsp salt
1/8 tsp ground black pepper
1 C. shredded Cheddar cheese

Directions

1. Set your oven to 350 degrees before doing anything else.
2. Get a baking dish and toast your nuts in the oven for 9 mins.
3. Microwave the broccoli until soft, then add in some pepper and salt.
4. Now stir fry your garlic and onions in butter for 4 mins then add in the broth and rice. Get everything boiling, then place a lid on the pot, and let the contents, gently cook over a lower level of heat for 9 mins.
5. On each serving plate add a layer of rice, then some broccoli, then nuts, and finally some cheese.
6. Enjoy.

Buttery
Parsley and Shrimp

Prep Time: 15 mins

Total Time: 35 mins

Servings per Recipe: 4

Calories	551 kcal
Fat	23 g
Carbohydrates	40.2g
Protein	38.5 g
Cholesterol	282 mg
Sodium	322 mg

Ingredients

1 C. brown rice
1 2/3 C. water
3 tbsps butter
3 tbsps olive oil
2 cloves garlic, minced
1/2 C. white wine
2 tbsps fresh lemon juice
1 1/2 lbs medium shrimp - peeled and
deveined

1/4 C. chopped fresh flat-leaf parsley
1/2 tsp cornstarch

Directions

1. Boil your water and rice. Once everything is boiling set the heat to low, and let the contents gently cook for 27 mins.
2. Stir fry your garlic in butter for 4 mins then add the lemon juice and wine.
3. Get the mix simmering then pour in the shrimp and cook for 8 mins. Now top everything with parsley and cook for 3 more mins.
4. Grab your cornstarch and gradually pour it in while stirring and cooking for about 1 to 2 mins until you have made a thick sauce.
5. Place your rice on a plate then top with the shrimp and sauce.
6. Enjoy.

ONIONS, CHICKEN, Peas, and Garlic Brown Rice

Prep Time: 20 mins
Total Time: 35 mins

Servings per Recipe: 3
Calories	486 kcal
Fat	13.7 g
Carbohydrates	57.4g
Protein	32.1 g
Cholesterol	64 mg
Sodium	720 mg

Ingredients

2 tbsps vegetable oil, divided
8 oz. skinless, boneless chicken breast,
cut into strips
1/2 red bell pepper, chopped
1/2 C. green onion, chopped
4 cloves garlic, minced
3 C. cooked brown rice

2 tbsps light soy sauce
1 tbsp rice vinegar
1 C. frozen peas, thawed

Directions

1. Stir fry your garlic, chicken, onions, and bell peppers in half of the veggie oil for 7 mins or until the chicken is fully done.
2. Place the chicken mix to the side.
3. Add in the rest of the oil and toast your rice in it for 1 min then add: peas, vinegar, and soy sauce.
4. Cook for 2 more mins and add back in the chicken.
5. Once everything is heated through you can serve it.
6. Enjoy.

Eggplant,
Basil, Feta Sandwich

Prep Time: 20 mins
Total Time: 30 mins

Servings per Recipe: 2
Calories	802 kcal
Fat	39.5 g
Carbohydrates	91.3g
Protein	23.8 g
Cholesterol	44 mg
Sodium	1460 mg

Ingredients

1 small eggplant, halved and sliced
1 tbsp olive oil, or as needed
1/4 C. mayonnaise
2 cloves garlic, minced
2 (6 inch) French sandwich rolls
1 small tomato, sliced
1/2 C. crumbled feta cheese
1/4 C. minced fresh basil leaves

Directions

1. Turn on your broiler to low if possible.
2. Get a bowl, mix: garlic and mayo.
3. Take your eggplant pieces and coat them with olive oil. Put them on a sheet for baking.
4. For 10 mins cook the eggplant in the broiler 6 inches from the heat.
5. Cut your French bread in half and toast it.
6. Spread a good amount of mayo and garlic mix on your bread and layer the following to form a sandwich: tomato, basil leaves, eggplant, and feta.
7. Enjoy.

BALSAMIC
Mushroom
Sandwich

Prep Time: 8 mins
Total Time: 20 mins

Servings per Recipe: 4
Calories	445 kcal
Fat	33.4 g
Carbohydrates	31.4g
Protein	7.8 g
Cholesterol	5 mg
Sodium	426 mg

Ingredients

2 cloves garlic, minced
6 tbsps olive oil
1/2 tsp dried thyme
2 tbsps balsamic vinegar
salt and pepper to taste
4 large Portobello mushroom caps
4 hamburger buns

1 tbsp capers
1/4 C. mayonnaise
1 tbsp capers, drained
1 large tomato, sliced
4 leaves lettuce

Directions

1. Preheat your broiler and set its rack so that it is near the heating source before doing anything else.
2. Get a bowl and mix: pepper, garlic, salt, olive oil, vinegar, and thyme.
3. Get a 2nd bowl, combine: mayo and capers.
4. Coat your mushrooms with half of the dressing.
5. Then toast the veggies for 5 mins under the broiler.
6. Flip the mushrooms after coating the opposite side with the remaining dressing.
7. Toast everything for 5 more mins.
8. Now also toast your bread.
9. Apply some mayo to the bread before layering a mushroom, some lettuce and tomato.
10. Enjoy.

Meatball
Madness Sandwich

Prep Time: 20 mins

Total Time: 40 mins

Servings per Recipe: 4

Calories	781 kcal
Fat	31.9 g
Carbohydrates	78.2g
Protein	43.6 g
Cholesterol	141 mg
Sodium	1473 mg

Ingredients

1 lb ground beef
3/4 C. bread crumbs
2 tsps dried Italian seasoning
2 cloves garlic, minced
2 tbsps minced fresh parsley
2 tbsps grated Parmesan cheese
1 egg, beaten
1 French baguette

1 tbsp extra-virgin olive oil
1/2 tsp garlic powder
1 pinch salt, or to taste
1 (14 oz.) jar spaghetti sauce
4 slices provolone cheese

Directions

1. Set your oven to 350 degrees before doing anything else.
2. Get a bowl, combine: eggs, beef, parmesan, bread crumbs, parsley, garlic, and Italian seasoning.
3. Mold the mix into your preferred size of meatballs and cook them in the oven for 22 mins.
4. Now cut your bread and take out some of the inside so the meatballs fit better.
5. Toast the bread for 6 mins in the oven after coating it with some olive oil, salt, and garlic powder.
6. Get a saucepan and heat up your pasta sauce.
7. Add in your meatballs to the sauce after they are cooked and mix everything.
8. Put some meatballs into your bread and then toast the sandwich in the oven for 4 mins before serving.
9. Enjoy.

ASIAN
Curry Squash Soup

Prep Time: 20 mins
Total Time: 1 hr 40 mins

Servings per Recipe: 12
Calories	160 kcal
Fat	11.1 g
Carbohydrates	19.3g
Protein	3.4 g
Cholesterol	< 1 mg
Sodium	< 310 mg

Ingredients

2 tbsp olive oil
2 chili moritas, or smoked jalapeno peppers, or any chipotle peppers
1 large white onion, diced
5 carrots, peeled and diced
2 stalks celery, diced
2 cloves garlic
salt and ground black pepper to taste
2 tbsp red curry paste, see appendix
1 tbsp smoked paprika
1 large butternut squash - peeled,

seeded, and diced
1 quart chicken stock
1 quart water
1 (14 oz.) can coconut milk
2 bay leaves

Directions

1. In a large heavy-bottom pan, heat the oil on medium-high heat and sauté the chili moritas for about 3-5 minutes.
2. Stir in the onion, carrots, celery, garlic, salt and pepper and cook for about 10-15 minutes.
3. Stir in the curry paste and butternut squash and cook for about 5 minutes.
4. Add the chicken stock, water, coconut milk and bay leaves and bring to a boil.
5. Reduce the heat and simmer for about 1 hour.
6. Remove from the heat and keep aside to cool slightly.
7. In a blender, add the squash mixture in batches and Cover and pulse till smooth.
8. Serve immediately

Complex
Thai Shrimp Curry

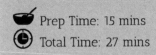 Prep Time: 15 mins

Total Time: 27 mins

Servings per Recipe: 4	
Calories	567.2
Fat	25.1 g
Cholesterol	143.2 mg
Sodium	1419.2 mg
Carbohydrates	68.5 g
Protein	18.8 g

Ingredients

2 tbsp peanut oil
1/2 C. chopped shallot
1 large red bell pepper, cut into strips
2 medium carrots, trimmed and shredded
2 tsp minced garlic
1 1/2 tbsp Thai red curry paste, see appendix
2 tbsp fish sauce
2 tsp light brown sugar

1 (14 oz.) can coconut milk
1 lb medium shrimp, peeled and deveined
3 tbsp chopped Thai basil
3 tbsp chopped fresh cilantro leaves
cooked jasmine rice, accompaniment
1 sprig fresh cilantro, garnish

Directions

1. In a large wok, heat the oil over medium-high heat and stir fry the shallots, bell peppers, carrots and garlic for about 2-3 minutes.
2. Add the curry paste and sauté for about 30-60 seconds.
3. Stir in the fish sauce, sugar and coconut milk and bring to a boil.
4. Simmer for about 2 minutes.
5. Add the shrimp and cook for about 2 minutes.
6. Remove from the heat and stir in the basil and cilantro.
7. Serve this curry over the jasmine rice and serve with a garnishing of the cilantro sprigs.

INDONESIAN INSPIRED
Beef Curry

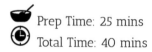

Prep Time: 25 mins
Total Time: 40 mins

Servings per Recipe: 4	
Calories	364.8
Fat	18 g
Cholesterol	69.7 mg
Sodium	450.3 mg
Carbohydrates	11.7 g
Protein	39.1 g

Ingredients

Curry Paste
5 dried red chilies
1 tbsp dried galangal, chopped
1 tbsp kaffir lime leaf, dried, chopped
1 C. water
2 green onions, chopped
2 garlic cloves, rushed
2 tsp lemon rind, grated
1 tbsp lemongrass, chopped
1 tsp ginger, grated
Stir-fry

1 tbsp oil
1 1/2 lb. flank steaks
6 oz. bamboo shoots, drained & sliced
into smaller pieces if necessary
1 fresh red chili, chopped
1 fresh green chili, chopped
1 tbsp fish sauce
1 kaffir lime leaf, dried
1 tsp brown sugar
2 tbsp fresh basil, chopped

Directions

1. For the curry paste in a bowl, add the water and soak the chilis, galangal and lime leaf for about 1-2 hours.
2. Drain the galangal mixture, reserving 1/2 C. of the soaking liquid.
3. In a food processor, add the galangal mixture, reserved liquid, green onions, garlic, lemon rind, lemon grass and ginger and pulse till smooth.
4. In a large deep pan, heat the oil and stir fry the steak till browned completely.
5. Add 1/2 C. of curry paste and stir fry for about 2 minutes.
6. Add the bamboo shoots, chilies, fish sauce, lime leaf and sugar and stir fry till the steak becomes tender.
7. Stir in the basil and serve over the white sticky rice.

Sweet Potato
Ginger Veggie Curry

Prep Time: 10 mins
Total Time: 30 mins

Servings per Recipe: 4	
Calories	441.7
Fat	17 g
Cholesterol	0 mg
Sodium	427.8 mg
Carbohydrates	71.7 g
Protein	2.9 g

Ingredients

2 sweet potatoes, peeled and in 1/2 cubes
1 onion, Chopped
3 garlic cloves, Finely chopped
2 inches fresh ginger, Finely chopped
olive oil, for sauté
1 tbsp red curry paste, see appendix
1 1/2 tbsp traditional curry paste, see appendix

1 (14 oz.) can coconut milk
1 chili (fresh and finely chopped)
fresh spinach (2 bags of the prepackaged spinach)
1 tbsp fish sauce
cilantro, for garnish

Directions

1. In a large pan, heat the oil on medium heat and sauté the onion, garlic and ginger till translucent.
2. Stir in the sweet potato and both pastes and cook till heated through.
3. Stir in the coconut milk and chili and cook till heated through.
4. Add the spinach and cook, covered for about 5 minutes, without stirring.
5. Stir in the fish sauce and simmer, covered for 5-10 minutes.
6. Serve this curry over the rice with a topping of the cilantro sprig.

COUNTRY
Curried Cabbage

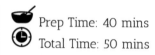 Prep Time: 40 mins

Total Time: 50 mins

Servings per Recipe: 8	
Calories	140 kcal
Fat	11.1 g
Carbohydrates	10.5g
Protein	2.4 g
Cholesterol	8 mg
Sodium	127 mg

Ingredients

1 tbsp olive oil
2 tbsp butter
1 small yellow onion, thinly sliced
1 C. julienned carrots
1 clove garlic, minced
1 small head cabbage, sliced
1/2 C. fresh shredded coconut
2 tbsp Indian curry powder
3/4 C. coconut milk

salt and pepper to taste
1/4 C. diced fresh tomato
1/4 C. chopped green onions
1/4 C. chopped cilantro

Directions

1. In a large skillet, heat the oil and butter on high heat and sauté the onion, carrot and garlic for about 1 minute.
2. Add the cabbage, coconut and curry powder and stir fry for about 2 minutes.
3. Reduce the heat to medium-low and stir in the coconut milk, salt and pepper.
4. Cook, covered till desired doneness of the curry.
5. Serve with a topping of the tomato, green onions and cilantro.

October's
Pumpkin Curried Soup

Prep Time: 20 mins
Total Time: 50 mins

Servings per Recipe: 6
Calories	171 kcal
Fat	13.5 g
Carbohydrates	12g
Protein	2 g
Cholesterol	0 mg
Sodium	601 mg

Ingredients

1/4 C. coconut oil
1 C. chopped onions
1 clove garlic, minced
3 C. vegetable broth
1 tsp curry powder
1/2 tsp salt
1/4 tsp ground coriander
1/4 tsp crushed red pepper flakes

1 (15 oz.) can 100% pure pumpkin
1 C. light coconut milk

Directions

1. In a deep pan, melt the coconut oil on medium-high heat and sauté the onion for about 5 minutes.
2. Stir in the vegetable broth, curry powder, salt, coriander and red pepper flakes and bring to a gentle boil.
3. Boil for about 10 minutes.
4. Cook, covered for about 15-20 minutes, stirring occasionally.
5. Stir in the pumpkin and coconut milk and cook for about 5 minutes.
6. Remove from the heat and keep aside to cool slightly.
7. In a blender, add the soup in batches and pulse till smooth.
8. Return the soup to pan on medium heat and cook till heated completely.

TOFU
Curry 101

Prep Time: 15 mins
Total Time: 45 mins

Servings per Recipe: 4
Calories	700 kcal
Fat	49.2 g
Carbohydrates	44.9 g
Protein	31.3 g
Cholesterol	0 mg
Sodium	1264 mg

Ingredients

4 slices fresh ginger root
4 cloves garlic, minced
1/4 C. cashews
2 stalks lemon grass, chopped
2 onions, sliced
3 tbsp olive oil
1 dash crushed red pepper flakes
2 tbsp curry powder
2 1/2 C. cubed firm tofu

1 (14 oz.) can coconut milk
14 fluid oz. water
2 medium potatoes, peeled and cubed
2 tsp salt
1 tbsp white sugar

Directions

1. In a food processor, add the ginger root, garlic, cashews, lemon grass and onions and pulse till a paste forms.
2. In a medium wok, heat the olive oil on low heat and stir in the ginger mixture and red pepper flakes.
3. Slowly, add the curry powder, stirring continuously.
4. Add the tofu and cook till heated completely.
5. Stir in the coconut milk, water and potatoes and bring to a boil.
6. Reduce the heat and simmer for about 20 minutes, stirring occasionally.
7. Stir in the salt and sugar and remove from the heat.

Kerala
Fish Curry

Prep Time: 15 mins

Total Time: 40 mins

Servings per Recipe: 2

Calories	237 kcal
Fat	14.2 g
Carbohydrates	18.7g
Protein	12.3 g
Cholesterol	18 mg
Sodium	51 mg

Ingredients

1 1/2 tsp curry powder
1/2 tsp ground ginger
1/4 tsp ground turmeric
1/4 tsp olive oil
3 cloves garlic, minced
1 onion, chopped
4 1/4 oz. coconut milk, divided
4 1/4 oz. water, divided

3 1/2 oz. cod, cut into bite-size pieces
1 large tomato, diced

Directions

1. In a skillet, add the curry powder, ground ginger and ground turmeric on medium heat and toast for about 5 minutes.
2. Add the olive oil and garlic and stir to combine well.
3. Add the onion and cook for about 5-7 minutes.
4. Stir in the about half of the coconut milk and half of the water and simmer for about 5 minutes.
5. Add the cod and simmer for about 5 minutes.
6. Add the tomato, remaining coconut milk and remaining water and simmer for about 5 minutes.

JAMAICAN STYLE
Shrimp Curry

Prep Time: 10 mins
Total Time: 35 mins

Servings per Recipe: 4

Calories	191 kcal
Fat	6.1 g
Carbohydrates	8.5g
Protein	24 g
Cholesterol	173 mg
Sodium	175 mg

Ingredients

1 tsp canola oil
1/2 C. minced onion
1/2 C. minced red bell pepper
1 clove garlic, minced
1 tsp ground cumin
3/4 tsp ground coriander
1/2 tsp curry powder
1/2 C. light coconut milk
1 tsp sugar

1/4 tsp crushed red pepper flakes
1 lb. jumbo shrimp, peeled and deveined
1 tbsp cornstarch
1 tbsp water
2 tbsp chopped fresh cilantro

Directions

1. In a large skillet, heat the oil on medium heat and sauté the onion, red pepper and garlic for about 3 minutes.
2. Stir in the cumin, coriander and curry powder and sauté for about 1 minute.
3. Stir in the coconut milk, sugar and crushed red pepper flakes and bring to a boil.
4. Reduce the heat and simmer, uncovered for about 2 minutes.
5. Stir in the shrimp and increase the heat to medium-high.
6. Cook for about 4 minutes, stirring occasionally.
7. In a small bowl, dissolve the cornstarch in 1 tbsp of the water.
8. Add the cornstarch mixture in the curry and stir to combine.
9. Cook for about 1 minute.
10. Stir in the cilantro and serve.

Alternative
Pumpkin Curry

Prep Time: 30 mins
Total Time: 1 hr

Servings per Recipe: 4
Calories	266 kcal
Fat	14.1 g
Carbohydrates	21.2g
Protein	17.5 g
Cholesterol	42 mg
Sodium	70 mg

Ingredients

2 skinless, boneless chicken breast halves - cut into small chunks
1 tsp poultry seasoning
1 tbsp olive oil
1 (2 lb.) sugar pumpkin -- peeled, seeded and cubed
1 tbsp butter
1 onion, chopped
2 cloves garlic, chopped
1 (1 inch) piece fresh ginger root, finely chopped

1 tbsp ground coriander
1 tbsp ground cumin
1 pinch ground turmeric
1 tsp red pepper flakes
1/2 C. canned coconut milk
1 1/2 C. chicken broth
salt to taste

Directions

1. Season the chicken pieces with the poultry seasoning evenly.
2. In a large skillet, heat the oil on medium heat and stir fry the chicken pieces till browned completely.
3. Remove from the heat and keep aside.
4. In another large skillet, melt the butter on medium heat and sauté the onion, garlic and ginger till the onion is translucent.
5. Stir in the coriander, cumin, turmeric and red pepper flakes and sauté till fragrant.
6. Add the pumpkin, cooked chicken, coconut milk, chicken broth and salt and cook for about 15-20 minutes.
7. Serve this curry over the rice or noodles.

SEAFOOD
Curry Dinner

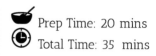 Prep Time: 20 mins

Total Time: 35 mins

Servings per Recipe: 6

Calories	166 kcal
Fat	10.9 g
Carbohydrates	7.8g
Protein	8.9 g
Cholesterol	31 mg
Sodium	238 mg

Ingredients

2 tbsp vegetable oil
1 medium onion, halved and sliced
1 tbsp minced fresh ginger root
1 tbsp minced garlic
1 (14 oz.) can light coconut milk
3 tbsp lime juice
1 tbsp curry paste, see appendix
1 tbsp brown sugar
12 medium shrimp, peeled (tails left on)
and deveined
12 sea scallops, halved
6 oz. asparagus, cut into 2-inch pieces
2 tbsp chopped cilantro
salt to taste

Directions

1. In a large skillet, heat the oil on medium-high heat and sauté the onion, ginger and garlic for about 2-3 minutes.

2. Stir in the coconut milk, lime juice, curry paste and brown sugar and bring to a gentle boil.

3. Cook for about 5 minutes.

4. Stir in the shrimp, scallops, asparagus, cilantro and salt and cook for about 5 minutes.

South Indian
Prawn Curry

Prep Time: 15 mins

Total Time: 45 mins

Servings per Recipe: 6

Calories	269 kcal
Fat	11.8 g
Carbohydrates	22g
Protein	17.9 g
Cholesterol	129 mg
Sodium	166 mg

Ingredients

1/2 C. rice flour
1/2 tsp ground turmeric
salt to taste
1 lb. peeled and deveined prawns
3 tbsp cooking oil
1 tsp cumin seeds
2 large onions, sliced thin
2 green chili peppers, halved lengthwise
1 tbsp ginger-garlic paste
3 C. pureed tomato
1/2 tsp Kashmiri red chili powder

1/2 tsp garam masala
1/2 tsp ground cumin
1/4 C. heavy cream (optional)
1/4 C. chopped fresh cilantro

Directions

1. In a bowl, mix together the rice flour, turmeric and salt.
2. Add the prawns and coat with the flour mixture evenly.
3. In a large skillet, heat 3 tbsp of the oil on medium heat and sauté the cumin seeds till they pop.
4. Add the onions, green chili peppers and ginger-garlic paste and sauté for about 5 minutes.
5. Stir in the pureed tomato, Kashmiri red chili powder, garam masala, ground cumin and salt and cook for about 10-15 minutes.
6. Add the cream and stir to combine.
7. Add the prawns and cook for about 3-5 minutes.
8. Serve with a garnishing of the cilantro.

THAI
Sardine Curry

Prep Time: 5 mins
Total Time: 15 mins

Servings per Recipe: 1
Calories	416 kcal
Fat	29.8 g
Carbohydrates	12.5g
Protein	24.6 g
Cholesterol	131 mg
Sodium	760 mg

Ingredients

1 tbsp canola oil
1 tbsp Thai red curry paste, see appendix
1 clove garlic, minced
1 shallot, minced

1 tbsp unsweetened coconut cream
1 (3.75 oz.) can sardines in oil, drained

Directions

1. In a large skillet, heat the oil and stir in the red curry paste.
2. Add the garlic and shallot and sauté till fragrant.
3. Add the sardines and cook till the skin becomes brown a little bit, tossing occasionally.
4. Gently, stir in the coconut cream and toss to coat well.
5. Bring to a boil and cook for about 5 minutes.

Rustic
Country Squash Pancakes

🥣 Prep Time: 15 mins
🕐 Total Time: 30 mins

Servings per Recipe: 8	
Calories	107 kcal
Fat	5.7 g
Carbohydrates	10.6g
Protein	3.9 g
Cholesterol	49 mg
Sodium	255 mg

Ingredients

2 tbsp chicken stock
2 eggs, slightly beaten
1 C. baking mix (such as Bisquick(R))
4 pattypan squash, grated
1/4 C. diced onion
1/4 C. grated Parmesan cheese

1 tsp minced garlic
1/2 C. vegetable oil

Directions

1. In a bowl, add the chicken stock and eggs and beat to combine.
2. Add the baking mix and beat till just moistened.
3. Add the squash, onion, Parmesan cheese and garlic and stir till well combined.
4. Keep aside for about 5 minutes.
5. In a large skillet, heat the oil to 350 degrees F.
6. Add about 1/4 C. of the mixture into the hot oil and cook for about 2-3 minutes per side.
7. Repeat with the remaining mixture.
8. Transfer pancakes to a brown paper bag-lined surface to drain.

FRENCH BEAN
and Parmesan Casserole

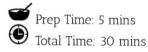

Prep Time: 5 mins
Total Time: 30 mins

Servings per Recipe: 4

Calories	421 kcal
Carbohydrates	59.8 g
Cholesterol	6 mg
Fat	13.7 g
Protein	16.8 g
Sodium	1013 mg

Ingredients

2 tbsps olive oil
1 large onion, sliced
1 medium carrot, sliced
2 cloves garlic, finely chopped
1 tsp white sugar
1 red bell pepper, seeded and chopped
6 fresh mushrooms, sliced
1 tbsp all-purpose flour
1/2 C. water
1 tbsp tomato paste
1/2 tsp dried basil

1/4 tsp dried thyme
1 (14.5 oz.) can red kidney beans, drained
1/2 tsp salt
ground black pepper to taste
1/2 (1 lb) loaf French bread, cut into 1/2 inch thick slices
1 tbsp olive oil
1/4 C. grated Parmesan cheese

Directions

1. Set your oven to 450 degrees F before doing anything else.
2. Cook onion, carrot and garlic in hot olive oil for a few minutes before adding mushrooms, sugar and red pepper, and cooking until you see that the onion is brown.
3. Add flour and cook for 1 minute before adding tomato paste, thyme, water, basil, beans, salt and pepper, and transferring all this to a baking dish.
4. Spread slices of bread dipped in oil over the mixture before spreading parmesan cheese.
5. Bake in the preheated oven for about 15 minutes.
6. Serve.

Turkey Soup

🥣 Prep Time: 20 mins
🕐 Total Time: 2 hrs 25 mins

Servings per Recipe: 8
Calories	234
Fat	13.5g
Cholesterol	106mg
Sodium	218mg
Carbohydrates	4.6g
Protein	18.5g

Ingredients

12 C. water
3 turkey drumsticks
3 carrots, peeled and chopped
2 large onions, chopped
3 celery stalks, chopped
4 garlic cloves, chopped
1 tbsp olive oil
½ tsp dried rosemary, crushed
½ tsp dried thyme, crushed
½ tsp dried sage, crushed
½ tsp celery salt
1 tbsp salt
½ tsp freshly ground black pepper
2 C. dried egg noodles

Directions

1. In a larger soup pan, add water and drumsticks and bring to a boil on high heat.
2. Add remaining ingredients except noodles and stir to combine.
3. Again bring to a boil and reduce the heat to low,
4. Simmer, covered for about 2 hours. Transfer the drumsticks in a large bowl and let them cool.
5. After cooling pull the meat from bones. Then chop into bite sized pieces and stir into soup.
6. Meanwhile in another pan of salted boiling water, add noodles and cook for about 5 minutes or according to package's directions. Drain well.
7. Divide noodles in serving bowls evenly.
8. Pour hot soup over noodles and serve immediately.

LENTILS
from Morocco

Prep Time: 20 mins
Total Time: 2 hrs 5 mins

Servings per Recipe: 6
Calories	329 kcal
Fat	3.6 g
Carbohydrates	56.5g
Protein	18.3 g
Cholesterol	0 mg
Sodium	317 mgt

Ingredients

2 onions, chopped
2 cloves garlic, minced
1 tsp grated fresh ginger
6 C. water
1 C. red lentils
1 (15 oz.) can garbanzo beans, drained
1 (19 oz.) can cannellini beans
1 (14.5 oz.) can diced tomatoes
1/2 C. diced carrots
1/2 C. chopped celery
1 tsp garam masala

1 1/2 tsps ground cardamom
1/2 tsp ground cayenne pepper
1/2 tsp ground cumin
1 tbsp olive oil

Directions

1. Stir fry the following, in a saucepan, in olive oil, for 7 mins: ginger, garlic, and onions.
2. Pour in your water, cumin, lentils, cayenne, chick peas, cardamom, kidney beans, masala, tomatoes, celery, and carrots.
3. Get the mix boiling, then lower the heat for a gentle simmer for 2 hrs.
4. Puree about one half of the soup in a blender and then mix it back into the saucepan before serving.
5. Enjoy.

Artisan Style Shiitake Mushrooms and Lentils

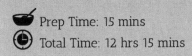

Prep Time: 15 mins
Total Time: 12 hrs 15 mins

Servings per Recipe: 8	
Calories	213 kcal
Fat	1.2 g
Carbohydrates	43.9g
Protein	8.4 g
Cholesterol	0 mg
Sodium	466 mg

Ingredients

2 quarts vegetable broth
2 C. sliced fresh button mushrooms
1 oz. dried shiitake mushrooms, torn into pieces
3/4 C. uncooked pearl barley
3/4 C. dry lentils
1/4 C. dried onion flakes
2 tsps minced garlic
2 tsps dried summer savory

3 bay leaves
1 tsp dried basil
2 tsps ground black pepper
salt to taste

Directions

1. Add the following to a crock pot: salt, broth, pepper, mushrooms, basil, barley, bay leaves, lentils, savory, onion flakes, and garlic. Place a lid on the slow cook and cook for 6 hrs on high or 12 hrs on low.

2. Enjoy.

RUSTIC LENTILS
with Savory Chicken

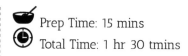

Prep Time: 15 mins
Total Time: 1 hr 30 tmins

Servings per Recipe: 6
Calories	308 kcal
Fat	13.5 g
Carbohydrates	18.7g
Protein	27.8 g
Cholesterol	68 mg
Sodium	816 mg

Ingredients

1 tbsp olive oil
2 lbs bone-in chicken pieces
1 large onion, finely chopped
1 small carrot, finely chopped
2 cloves garlic, finely chopped
3/4 C. dried lentils
1 (14 oz.) can chicken broth
1/2 tsp salt
1 (10 oz.) can tomato sauce

1/2 tsp dried rosemary
1/2 tsp dried basil
1 tbsp lemon juice

Directions

1. Stir fry your chicken, in oil, in a big pot for 6 mins per side and then place the chicken to the side.
2. Now stir fry your onions for 6 mins in the same pan and then add in the garlic, lentils, salt, broth, and carrots.
3. Get everything boiling and then place a lid on the pot and cook for 22 mins over low heat.
4. Now add back in, your chicken, and let the contents keep simmering for 20 more mins with a lid on the pot.
5. Add water if needed then add in your tomato sauce, basil, and rosemary.
6. Let the tomato sauce cook for 10 mins and finally combine in the lemon juice.
7. Enjoy.

Sunbelt
Quinoa Classic

🥣 Prep Time: 10 mins
🕐 Total Time: 40 mins

Servings per Recipe: 3	
Calories	233 kcal
Fat	18.9 g
Carbohydrates	10.5g
Protein	6.1 g
Cholesterol	13 mg
Sodium	49 mg

Ingredients

1/4 C. quinoa
3 tbsps olive oil
2 tbsps raw sunflower seeds
2 cloves garlic, minced
1/2 C. fresh spinach leaves

2 tsps lemon juice
1/3 C. grated goat gouda cheese

Directions

1. Boil your quinoa in salt and water for 17 mins. Then with a strainer remove all the liquid and clean the quinoa under cold water.
2. Toast your sunflower seeds in olive oil for 3 mins then add the garlic and cook for 3 more mins.
3. Pour in your quinoa and also the spinach. Stir and heat everything until the spinach is soft.
4. Now add your lemon juice and some cheese.
5. Continue stirring for a few more mins until the cheese is melted.
6. When serving this dish top with more cheese.
7. Enjoy.

LENTIL SOUP
(Jalapenos, Black Beans, and Peppers)

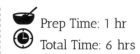 Prep Time: 1 hr
Total Time: 6 hrs

Servings per Recipe: 10
Calories	231 kcal
Fat	1.2 g
Carbohydrates	43.4g
Protein	12.6 g
Cholesterol	0 mg
Sodium	851 mg

Ingredients

1 lb dry black beans
1 1/2 quarts water
1 carrot, chopped
1 stalk celery, chopped
1 large red onion, chopped
6 cloves garlic, crushed
2 green bell peppers, chopped
2 jalapeno pepper, seeded and minced
1/4 C. dry lentils
1 (28 oz.) can peeled and diced tomatoes

2 tbsps chili powder
2 tsps ground cumin
1/2 tsp dried oregano
1/2 tsp ground black pepper
3 tbsps red wine vinegar
1 tbsp salt
1/2 C. uncooked white rice

Directions

1. Submerge your beans in about 3 times their size of water.
2. Then get everything boiling for 12 mins.
3. Now place a lid on the pan and shut the heat.
4. Let the beans sit for 1 and a half hours before removing the liquid and then rinsing the beans.
5. Add your beans to a slow cooker with 1.5 quarts of fresh water and cook for 3 hrs on high.
6. Now add the following after 3 hrs of cooking: tomatoes, carrots, lentils, celery, salt, chili powder, vinegar, cumin, black pepper, and oregano, jalapenos, onions, bell peppers, and garlic.
7. With low heat cook for 3 more hrs. Then add the rice when about 25 mins is left in the cooking time.
8. Take half of the soup and puree it in a blender then put it back in the pot. Enjoy.

Quinoa Festival

🥣 Prep Time: 5 mins
🕐 Total Time: 40 mins

Servings per Recipe: 2	
Calories	473 kcal
Fat	19.8 g
Carbohydrates	62.8g
Protein	13.5 g
Cholesterol	0 mg
Sodium	48 mg

Ingredients

- 2 tbsps olive oil, or as needed
- 1 small onion, diced
- 2 cloves garlic, minced
- 1 C. quinoa
- 2 C. chicken broth
- 1 tbsp curry powder, or to taste
- 1 tbsp ancho chili powder
- salt and pepper to taste

Directions

1. Stir fry your garlic and onions in oil for 4 mins then add your quinoa and cook for 6 mins.
2. Add in the broth and get everything boiling. Once the quinoa is boiling, add your chili and curry powder, place a lid on the pot, and lower the heat. Let the contents cook for 27 mins.
3. Before serving add your preferred amount of pepper and salt.
4. Enjoy.

CHIPOTLE
Quinoa

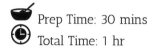 Prep Time: 30 mins

Total Time: 1 hr

Servings per Recipe: 10	
Calories	233 kcal
Fat	3.5 g
Carbohydrates	42g
Protein	11.5 g
Cholesterol	0 mg
Sodium	540 mg

Ingredients

1 C. uncooked quinoa, rinsed
2 C. water
1 tbsp vegetable oil
1 onion, chopped
4 cloves garlic, chopped
1 tbsp chili powder
1 tbsp ground cumin
1 (28 oz.) can crushed tomatoes
2 (19 oz.) cans black beans, rinsed and drained
1 green bell pepper, chopped

1 red bell pepper, chopped
1 zucchini, chopped
1 jalapeno pepper, seeded and minced
1 tbsp minced chipotle peppers in adobo sauce
1 tsp dried oregano
salt and ground black pepper to taste
1 C. frozen corn
1/4 C. chopped fresh cilantro

Directions

1. Boil your quinoa in water, then place a lid on the pot, lower the heat, and let the contents gently boil for 17 mins.
2. Simultaneously, in veggie oil, stir fry your onions for 7 mins then season them with: cumin, chili powder, and garlic.
3. Cook for 2 more mins before adding: oregano, tomatoes, chipotles, black beans, jalapenos, bell peppers, and zucchini.
4. Add in your preferred amount of black pepper and salt and get the contents to a gentle boil with high then low heat.
5. Place a lid on the pot and let the contents gently cook for 22 mins.
6. Now pour in your corn and quinoa and heat for 7 more mins before shutting the heat and topping with some cilantro.
7. Enjoy.

Squash and Garbanzos Couscous (Moroccan Style)

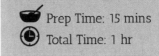 Prep Time: 15 mins

Total Time: 1 hr

Servings per Recipe: 4

Calories	502 kcal
Fat	11.7 g
Carbohydrates	93.8g
Protein	11.2 g
Cholesterol	10 mg
Sodium	728 mg

Ingredients

2 tbsps brown sugar
1 tbsp butter, melted
2 large acorn squash, halved and seeded
2 tbsps olive oil
2 cloves garlic, chopped
2 stalks celery, chopped
2 carrots, chopped
1 C. garbanzo beans, drained
1/2 C. raisins

1 1/2 tbsps ground cumin
salt and pepper to taste
1 (14 oz.) can chicken broth
1 C. uncooked couscous

Directions

1. Set your oven to 350 degrees before doing anything else.
2. Cook your squash for 32 mins in the oven. Then top the squash with a mix of butter and sugar that has been melted and stirred together.
3. Stir fry, for 7 mins, in olive oil: carrots, celery, and garlic.
4. Now add the raisins and beans.
5. Fry the contents until everything is soft then add in pepper, salt, and cumin.
6. Add the broth to the carrot mix and then add the couscous.
7. Place a lid on the pot and place the pot to the side away from all heat.
8. Let the contents sit for 7 mins.
9. Fill your squashes with the couscous mix.
10. Enjoy.

CHERRY TOMATOES,
Onions, and Basil
Couscous

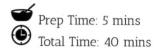

Prep Time: 5 mins
Total Time: 40 mins

Servings per Recipe: 4
Calories	299 kcal
Fat	12.4 g
Carbohydrates	38g
Protein	9.1 g
Cholesterol	6 mg
Sodium	196 mg

Ingredients

1 C. couscous
1 C. boiling water
3 tbsps olive oil
1 clove garlic, minced
1/4 C. diced red bell pepper
4 green onions, sliced
1 C. cherry tomatoes
1 C. fresh basil leaves

1 pinch salt
1 pinch ground black pepper
1 dash balsamic vinegar
1/4 C. grated Parmesan cheese

Directions

1. Set your oven to 350 degrees before doing anything else.
2. Get your water boiling then pour in your couscous.
3. Get everything boiling again. Then place a lid on the pot, shut the heat, and let the mix sit for 7 mins before stirring.
4. Simultaneously stir fry your peppers, onions, and garlic for 3 mins then add: pepper, tomatoes, salt, basil, and couscous.
5. Pour everything into a baking dish and add in your balsamic.
6. Cook everything in the oven for 25 mins then add the parmesan.
7. Enjoy.

Homemade
Piri Piri

Prep Time: 5 mins
Total Time: 1 hr 20 mins

Servings per Recipe: 1	
Calories	692.0
Fat	70.6g
Cholesterol	0.0mg
Sodium	2468.4mg
Carbohydrates	17.6g
Protein	3.4g

Ingredients

4 tbsps lemon juice
5 tbsps olive oil
1/4 C. vinegar
1 tbsp cayenne pepper
1 tbsp garlic, minced

1 tbsp paprika
1 tsp salt
1 tbsp chili flakes

Directions

1. Get a medium mixing bowl. Combine in it all the ingredients.
2. Use this sauce to coat you chicken with it before grilling or roasting it in the oven. Serve it warm.
3. Enjoy.

PORTO ALEGRE
Salsa

Prep Time: 10 mins
Total Time: 10 mins

Servings per Recipe: 2

Calories	112.4
Fat	7.0g
Cholesterol	0.0mg
Sodium	8.1mg
Carbohydrates	12.2g
Protein	1.7g

Ingredients

1 large onion, diced
1 large tomatoes, peeled, seeded and diced
2 tbsps red wine vinegar
2 garlic cloves, minced
1 - 2 tbsp olive oil
1 tsp dried parsley
3 drops chili sauce

salt, as needed
pepper, as needed

Directions

1. Get a large mixing bowl: Combine in it all the ingredients and stir them to coat.
2. Place the sauce in the fridge for sit for at least 1 h. Serve it right away.
3. Enjoy.

Collard Green
Skillet

Prep Time: 5 mins
Total Time: 25 mins

Servings per Recipe: 8	
Calories	78.4
Fat	5.2g
Cholesterol	3.8mg
Sodium	31.8mg
Carbohydrates	7.0g
Protein	2.6g

Ingredients

2 lbs collard greens
2 tbsps olive oil
1 tbsp butter
1/3 C. minced shallot
1 tbsp minced garlic

kosher salt and pepper

Directions

1. Remove the stems of the collard greens and slice them into thin strips.
2. Place a large skillet over medium heat. Melt the butter in it. Sauté in it the garlic with shallot for 2 min.
3. Stir in the collard greens and cook them for 12 to 14 min or until they are done. Adjust the seasoning of your stir fry then serve it warm.
4. Enjoy.

CHICKEN TAQUITOS
and Homemade Guacamole

 Prep Time: 15 mins
Total Time: 25 mins

Servings per Recipe: 1
Calories   228.0
Fat   11.0g
Cholesterol   30.4mg
Sodium   245.7mg
Carbohydrates   19.3g
Protein   13.2g

Ingredients

3 C. shredded cooked chicken
2 tsps lemon juice
1 tsp cumin
1 jalapeno, diced
2 tbsps chopped cilantro
2 garlic cloves, minced
1/2 C. Monterey jack cheese, shredded
salt and pepper
12 small flour tortillas
oil

2 avocados, diced
1/2 small red onion, diced
1 jalapeno, diced
4 tbsps cilantro, chopped
2 tsps lemon juice
1/2 C. cherry tomatoes, halved
salt and pepper

Directions

1. To make the taquitos:
2. Get a large mixing bowl: Mix in it the chicken with lemon juice, cumin, jalapeno, cilantro, cheese, garlic, a pinch of salt and pepper. Place it aside to sit for 20 min.
3. Lay a tortilla on a cookie sheet and place it in on the side of it in a long line 2 tbsps of the filling.
4. Roll the tortilla over the filling in the shape of a cigar and place it in a lined up baking sheet. Repeat the process with remaining ingredients.
5. Place a heavy pan over medium heat. Heat 1/4 inch of oil in it. Lay in it the taquitos gently and cook them for 2 to 4 min or until they become golden brown.
6. Remove the taquitos from the hot oil and place them aside.
7. To make the guacamole:
8. Get a mixing bowl: Combine in it all the ingredients and mix them well. Serve your taquitos warm with the guacamole.
9. Enjoy.

Easy
Homemade Churrasco

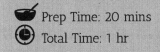 Prep Time: 20 mins

Total Time: 1 hr

Servings per Recipe: 4	
Calories	583.8
Fat	41.3g
Cholesterol	192.7mg
Sodium	1860.5mg
Carbohydrates	5.8g
Protein	45.1g

Ingredients

2 lbs beef tenderloin
3 tsps salt
2 lemons, juice of
2 garlic cloves, mashed
1/4 tsp pepper

1/2 tsp crushed red pepper flakes
1 large onion, chopped
1/2 C. cilantro leaf

Directions

1. Get a small mixing bowl: Mix in it the juice of 1 lemon, garlic, salt and pepper.
2. Coat the tenderloin with the mix and wrap it with a piece of a plastic wrap. Place it in the fridge for an overnight.
3. Preheat the grill and grease it.
4. Drain the tenderloin with and grill until it is done to your liking.
5. Get a small mixing bowl: Mix in it the rest of the lemon juice, onion, cilantro and pepper flakes to make the salsa.
6. Serve your tenderloin warm with the onion salsa.
7. Enjoy.

BRAZILIAN
Long Grain

Prep Time: 10 mins
Total Time: 30 mins

Servings per Recipe: 4
Calories   462.3
Fat   6.3g
Cholesterol   5.4mg
Sodium   269.2mg
Carbohydrates   86.9g
Protein   12.4g

Ingredients

1 large onion, peeled and cut into
chunks
10 garlic cloves, peeled
1/2 C. fresh parsley leaves
1/2 C. fresh basil leaf
3 tbsps corn oil

2 C. long grain rice
salt and pepper, to taste
3 C. chicken stock

Directions

1. Get a food processor: Place in it the onion with garlic, parsley and basil. Process them until they become smooth.
2. Place a heavy saucepan over medium heat. Heat the oil in it. Cook in it the rice for 3 min.
3. Add 1 tbsp of the herbed onion mix with a pinch of salt and pepper. Cook them for 2 min.
4. Stir in the stock and cook them until they start boiling. Put on the lid and let them cook for 18 to 22 min or until the rice is done.
5. Fluff the rice with a fork. Add the remaining herbed onion mix and stir them to coat. Serve your warm salad.
6. Enjoy.

Classical
American Burger I (Spicy Chili Burger)

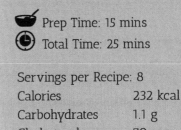

Prep Time: 15 mins
Total Time: 25 mins

Servings per Recipe: 8	
Calories	232 kcal
Carbohydrates	1.1 g
Cholesterol	70 mg
Fat	16.4 g
Protein	19.1 g
Sodium	67 mg

Ingredients

1 tsp ground cumin
2 tbsps chopped fresh cilantro
1 tsp crushed red pepper flakes
1 fresh habanero pepper, seeded and minced (optional)
1 small fresh poblano chile pepper, seeded and minced

2 fresh jalapeno peppers, seeded and minced
2 tsps minced garlic
2 lbs ground beef

Directions

1. Set grill or grilling plate at medium heat and put some oil before continuing.
2. Take out a large bowl and mix beef, jalapeno peppers, poblano pepper, garlic, red pepper flakes, cilantro, habanero pepper and cumin.
3. Make burger patties from this mixture and cook them on the heated grill for about 5 mins each side.
4. NOTE: If using a grilling plate then increase the cooking time of the meat until your appropriate tenderness has been achieved.

GOUDA
and Shrimp Cake

 Prep Time: 45 mins

Total Time: 1 hr 10 mins

Servings per Recipe: 12

Calories	701 kcal
Fat	56.3 g
Carbohydrates	22.7g
Protein	26.8 g
Cholesterol	248 mg
Sodium	1075 mg

Ingredients

1 tbsp olive oil
1 onion
6 tsps minced garlic
1 lb fresh shrimp, peeled and deveined
12 shells puff pastry, baked
4 tbsps butter or margarine
3 (8 oz.) packages cream cheese,
softened
4 eggs
1/2 C. heavy cream

16 oz. smoked Gouda, grated
2 tsps salt

Directions

1. Set your oven to 350 degrees before doing anything else.
2. Begin to stir fry your garlic and onions until the onions are see-through then place them to the side.
3. Place 12 pieces of shrimp to the side and dice the rest into half inch pieces.
4. Fry the shrimp for 5 mins.
5. Get a bowl and begin to whisk your cream cheese until it is fluffy then add in your eggs 1 by one.
6. Once the eggs are mixed in combine in the salt, cream, shrimp, Gouda, and onions.
7. Enter this mix into your pastry shells and cook everything in the oven for 30 mins.
8. Top the dish with some chives and the whole shrimp.
9. Enjoy.

Basil
Zucchini Bites

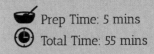 Prep Time: 5 mins

Total Time: 55 mins

Servings per Recipe: 10	
Calories	359 kcal
Fat	30.2 g
Carbohydrates	7.3g
Protein	16 g
Cholesterol	151 mg
Sodium	460 mg

Ingredients

8 tbsps grated Parmesan cheese
1/2 C. vegetable oil
1/2 C. sesame seeds
1 onion, chopped
1 clove garlic, minced
2 1/2 C. grated zucchini
6 eggs, beaten

1/3 C. dried bread crumbs
1/2 tsp salt
1/2 tsp dried basil
1/2 tsp dried oregano
1/4 tsp ground black pepper
3 C. shredded Cheddar cheese

Directions

1. Coat a casserole dish with oil and with 3 tbsp of parmesan.
2. Then set your oven to 325 degrees before doing anything else.
3. Begin to toast your sesame seeds in half a tsp of veggie oil.
4. Get a bowl, combine: cheddar, veggie oil, pepper, onion, oregano, garlic, basil, zucchini, salt, eggs, and bread crumbs.
5. Combine the mix until it is even then layer everything into the casserole dish.
6. Top the mix with the sesame seeds and parmesan.
7. Cook the dish in the oven for 35 mins.
8. Then cut it into servings once it has cooled off.
9. Enjoy.

GREEK
Moussaka I

Prep Time: 45 mins
Total Time: 1 hr 45 mins

Servings per Recipe: 8

Calories	567 kcal
Fat	39.4 g
Carbohydrates	29.1g
Protein	23.6 g
Cholesterol	123 mg
Sodium	1017 mg

Ingredients

3 eggplants, peeled and cut into 1/2 inch thick slices
salt
1/4 C. olive oil
1 tbsp butter
1 lb. lean ground beef
salt to taste
ground black pepper to taste
2 onions, chopped
1 clove garlic, minced
1/4 tsp ground cinnamon
1/4 tsp ground nutmeg
1/2 tsp fines herbs

2 tbsps dried parsley
1 (8 oz.) can tomato sauce
1/2 C. red wine
1 egg, beaten
4 C. milk
1/2 C. butter
6 tbsps all-purpose flour
salt to taste
ground white pepper, to taste
1 1/2 C. freshly grated Parmesan cheese
1/4 tsp ground nutmeg

Directions

1. On a working surface, layered with paper towels, lay out all your pieces of eggplant.
2. Top the eggplants with salt and let them sit for 40 mins.
3. Now sear the veggies in olive oil then place them on some new paper towels.
4. Top your beef with pepper and salt and then fry it in butter with the garlic and onions.
5. Once the beef is fully done add in: parsley, wine, cinnamon, tomato sauce, herbs, and nutmeg.
6. Let this all cook for 23 mins.
7. Let the mix cool off then add in the whisked eggs.
8. Get a casserole dish and coat it with nonstick spray then set your oven to 350 degrees before doing anything else.
9. Now get another pot and begin to heat your milk.

10. In a separate pan mix flour and butter together until smooth and set the heat to low.

11. Add in your milk slowly while stirring.

12. Continue heating and stirring until everything is thick.

13. Now add in the white pepper and some salt.

14. Place most of your eggplant in the dish and top the eggplants with: the veggies, the meat, half of your parmesan, more eggplant, and the rest of the cheese.

15. Cover everything with the milk sauce and then some nutmeg.

16. Cook the layers for 60 mins in the oven.

17. Then let the dish sit for 10 mins before serving.

18. Enjoy.

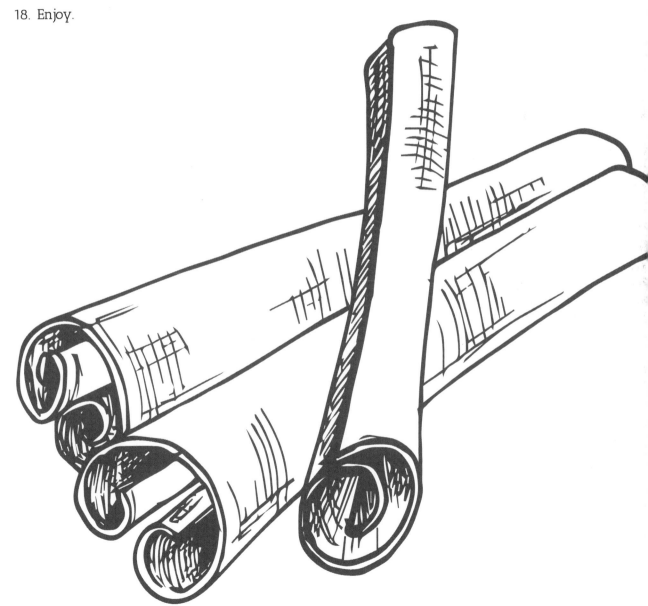

PASTA
from Athens

🍳 Prep Time: 15 mins
🕐 Total Time: 30 mins

Servings per Recipe: 12	
Calories	488 kcal
Fat	11.4 g
Carbohydrates	70g
Protein	32.6 g
Cholesterol	55 mg
Sodium	444 mg

Ingredients

1 (16 oz.) package linguine pasta
1/2 C. chopped red onion
1 tbsp olive oil
2 cloves garlic, crushed
1 lb. skinless, boneless chicken breast
meat - cut into bite-size pieces
1 (14 oz.) can marinated artichoke
hearts, drained and chopped
1 large tomato, chopped
1/2 C. crumbled feta cheese

3 tbsps chopped fresh parsley
2 tbsps lemon juice
2 tsps dried oregano
salt and pepper to taste
2 lemons, wedged, for garnish

Directions

1. Cook your pasta in water and salt for 9 mins then remove all the liquids.
2. Stir fry your garlic and onions in olive oil for 4 mins then add in the chicken and cook the mix until the chicken is fully done.
3. Now set the heat to low and add the following: pasta, artichokes, oregano, tomato, lemon juice, feta, and parsley.
4. Simmer this mix for 5 mins then shut the heat and add in pepper, salt, and lemon wedges.
5. Enjoy.

Mediterranean
Pasta

🥣 Prep Time: 20 mins
🕐 Total Time: 50 mins

Servings per Recipe: 10	
Calories	685 kcal
Fat	13.2 g
Carbohydrates	96.2g
Protein	47 g
Cholesterol	94 mg
Sodium	826 mg

Ingredients

1 (16 oz.) package penne pasta
1 1/2 tbsps butter
1/2 C. chopped red onion
2 cloves garlic, minced
1 lb. skinless, boneless chicken breast
halves - cut into bite-size pieces
1 (14 oz.) can artichoke hearts in water
1 tomato, chopped
1/2 C. crumbled feta cheese

3 tbsps chopped fresh parsley
2 tbsps lemon juice
1 tsp dried oregano
salt to taste
ground black pepper to taste

Directions

1. Boil your pasta in water and salt for 9 mins then remove all the liquids.
2. At the same time, stir fry your garlic and onions in butter for 4 mins, then combine in the chicken, and cook everything for 9 more mins.
3. Set the heat to a low level and add in your artichokes after chopping them and discarding their liquids.
4. Cook this mix for 3 more mins before adding in: pasta, tomatoes, oregano, feta, lemon juice, and the fresh parsley.
5. Cook everything for 4 mins to get it all hot. Then add in your pepper and salt after shutting the heat.
6. Enjoy.

GREEK
Spinach Puff Pastry Bake

🍲 Prep Time: 30 mins
🕐 Total Time: 1 hr 30 mins

Servings per Recipe: 5	
Calories	528 kcal
Fat	36.7 g
Carbohydrates	32.8g
Protein	21 g
Cholesterol	108 mg
Sodium	925 mg

Ingredients

3 tbsps olive oil
1 large onion, chopped
1 bunch green onions, chopped
2 cloves garlic, minced
2 lbs spinach, rinsed and chopped
1/2 C. chopped fresh parsley
2 eggs, lightly beaten

1/2 C. ricotta cheese
1 C. crumbled feta cheese
8 sheets phyllo dough
1/4 C. olive oil

Directions

1. Coat a baking pan with nonstick spray and then set your oven to 350 degrees before doing anything else.
2. Stir fry your garlic, onions, and green onions in olive oil for 4 mins. Then add in, the parsley and the spinach, and cook it all for 3 more mins.
3. Remove all the contents.
4. Get a bowl, combine: feta, onion mix, ricotta, and eggs.
5. Coat a piece of phyllo with olive oil then layer it in the pan.
6. Add another piece and also more olive oil.
7. Do this two more times.
8. Add your ricotta mix and fold the phyllo around the filling and seal it.
9. Cook everything in the oven for 35 mins.
10. Then cut the contents into your preferred shape.
11. Enjoy.

Classical Italian Pasta

Prep Time: 20 mins
Total Time: 55 mins

Servings per Recipe: 4
Calories	619 kcal
Fat	17.7 g
Carbohydrates	79.5g
Protein	31.2 g
Cholesterol	14 mg
Sodium	706 mg

Ingredients

2 tbsps olive oil
1 anchovy fillet
2 tbsps capers
3 cloves minced garlic
1/2 C. dry white wine
1/4 tsp dried oregano
1 pinch red pepper flakes, or to taste
3 C. crushed Italian (plum) tomatoes
salt and ground black pepper to taste
1 pinch cayenne pepper, or to taste

1 (7 oz.) can oil-packed tuna, drained
1/4 C. diced fresh flat-leaf parsley
1 (12 oz.) package spaghetti
1 tbsp extra-virgin olive oil, or to taste
1/4 C. freshly grated Parmigiano-Reggiano cheese, or to taste
1 tbsp diced fresh flat-leaf parsley, or to taste

Directions

1. Stir fry your capers and anchovies in olive oil for 4 mins then combine in the garlic and continue frying the mix for 2 more mins.
2. Now add: pepper flakes, white wine, and orange.
3. Stir the mix and turn up the heat.
4. Let the mix cook for 5 mins before adding the tomatoes and getting the mix to a gentle simmer.
5. Once the mix is simmering add in: cayenne, black pepper, and salt.
6. Set the heat to low and let everything cook for 12 mins.
7. Now begin to boil your pasta in water and salt for 10 mins then remove all the liquids and leave the noodles in the pan.
8. Combine the simmering tomatoes with the noodles and place a lid on the pot. With a low level of heat warm everything for 4 mins.
9. When serving your pasta top it with some Parmigiano-Reggiano, parsley, and olive oil.
10. Enjoy.

LASAGNA
Bakes

Prep Time: 40 mins
Total Time: 1 hr 40 mins

Servings per Recipe: 4

Calories	637 kcal
Fat	21.6 g
Carbohydrates	70.1g
Protein	44.3 g
Cholesterol	87 mg
Sodium	1281 mg

Ingredients

8 whole wheat lasagna noodles
1/2 lb ground turkey
6 cloves garlic, crushed
1 (10 oz.) package frozen diced spinach, thawed and drained
1/2 C. diced fresh chives
1/2 tsp dried oregano
1/2 tsp dried parsley
1/4 tsp dried basil
2 egg whites

1 (15 oz.) container reduced-fat ricotta cheese
2 tbsps crumbled low-fat feta cheese
2 tbsps grated Parmesan cheese
1/2 tsp ground black pepper
1 (28 oz.) jar low-fat tomato pasta sauce
1/2 C. shredded low-fat Cheddar cheese

Directions

1. Set your oven to 375 degrees before doing anything else.
2. Boil your pasta in water and salt for 9 mins then remove all the liquids.
3. Begin to stir fry your garlic and turkey for 12 mins and break the meat into pieces as it cooks.
4. Once the meat is fully done add in: the basil, spinach, parsley, oregano, and chives.
5. Stir the mix and cook everything for 60 more secs then shut the heat.
6. Get a bowl, combine: parmesan, egg whites, feta, and ricotta. Stir the mix then add in the black pepper and turkey mix.
7. On a working surface place a large piece of wax paper and lay out the pasta.
8. Form your cheese mix into eight balls and put one ball on each piece of lasagna and roll everything up into a burrito shape.
9. Continue this process with all of your noodles.
10. Now coat the bottom of a casserole dish with tomato sauce and then layer your lasagna rolls over the sauce with seam portion facing downwards in the sauce.

11. Top the rolls with the rest of the pasta sauce and a layering of cheddar.

12. Place a covering of foil around the dish and put everything in oven for 45 mins.

13. Enjoy.

ITALIAN STYLE
Rice

Prep Time: 15 mins
Total Time: 1 hr 20 mins

Servings per Recipe: 4
Calories	643 kcal
Fat	22.1 g
Carbohydrates	77.5g
Protein	30.9 g
Cholesterol	150 mg
Sodium	1025 mg

Ingredients

1 C. uncooked white rice
2 C. water
2 tsps olive oil
3 cloves garlic, finely diced
1/2 lb lean ground beef
salt and pepper to taste
1/2 C. tomato-based pasta sauce

1/2 C. grated Parmesan cheese
1/2 C. shredded mozzarella cheese
2 eggs, beaten
1 C. dry bread crumbs
1 1/2 C. tomato-based pasta sauce

Directions

1. Get your rice boiling in water, set the heat to low, place a lid on the pot, and let the rice cook for 22 mins.
2. Now begin to stir fry your garlic in olive oil for 5 mins then add in the beef.
3. Continue to fry the meat until it is fully done for 12 mins then remove any excess oils.
4. Get a bowl, combine: 1/2 C. pasta sauce, rice, pepper, beef, and salt.
5. Stir the mix then add in the mozzarella and parmesan.
6. Let the cheese melt, then using your hands, shape the mix into balls of about 2 inches.
7. Lay all the rice balls onto a cookie sheet.
8. Now set your oven to 350 degrees before doing anything else.
9. Place the rice balls into the fridge for 30 mins. Then coat the balls with whisked eggs and bread crumbs.
10. Place them back on the sheet and cook everything in the oven for 30 mins.
11. Now get 2.5 C. of tomato sauce hot while the rice balls cook and when they are done coat everything with the hot tomato sauce.
12. Enjoy.

Classical
Lasagna I

Prep Time: 30 mins
Total Time: 2 hrs

Servings per Recipe: 8
Calories	664 kcal
Fat	29.5 g
Carbohydrates	48.3g
Protein	50.9 g
Cholesterol	1168 mg
Sodium	1900 mg

Ingredients

1 1/2 lbs lean ground beef
1 onion, diced
2 cloves garlic, minced
1 tbsp diced fresh basil
1 tsp dried oregano
2 tbsps brown sugar
1 1/2 tsps salt
1 (29 oz.) can diced tomatoes
2 (6 oz.) cans tomato paste
12 dry lasagna noodles

2 eggs, beaten
1 pint part-skim ricotta cheese
1/2 C. grated Parmesan cheese
2 tbsps dried parsley
1 tsp salt
1 lb mozzarella cheese, shredded
2 tbsps grated Parmesan cheese

Directions

1. Stir fry your garlic, onions, and beef for 3 mins then combine in: tomato paste, basil, diced tomatoes, oregano, 1.5 tsp salt, and brown sugar.
2. Now set your oven to 375 degrees before doing anything else.
3. Begin to boil your pasta in water and salt for 9 mins then remove all the liquids.
4. Get a bowl, combine: 1 tsp salt, eggs, parsley, ricotta, and parmesan.
5. Place a third of the pasta in a casserole dish and top everything with half of the cheese mix, one third of the sauce, and 1/2 of the mozzarella.
6. Continue layering in this manner until all the ingredients have been used up.
7. Then top everything with some more parmesan.
8. Cook the lasagna in the oven for 35 mins.
9. Enjoy.

RESTAURANT STYLE
Primavera

Prep Time: 20 mins
Total Time: 50 mins

Servings per Recipe: 8
Calories	477 kcal
Fat	21.8 g
Carbohydrates	50.1g
Protein	20.5 g
Cholesterol	38 mg
Sodium	621 mg

Ingredients

1 (16 oz.) package uncooked farfalle
pasta
1 lb hot Italian turkey sausage, cut into
1/2 inch slices
1/2 C. olive oil, divided
4 cloves garlic, diced
1/2 onion, diced
2 small zucchini, diced
2 small yellow squash, diced
6 roma (plum) tomatoes, diced

1 green bell pepper, diced
20 leaves fresh basil
2 tsps chicken bouillon granules
1/2 tsp red pepper flakes
1/2 C. grated Parmesan cheese

Directions

1. Cook your pasta in water and salt for 9 mins then remove all the liquids.
2. Stir fry your sausage until fully done then remove it from the pan.
3. Now begin to stir fry your onions and garlic until the mix is hot then add in: basil, zucchini, bell peppers, squash, and tomatoes.
4. Stir the mix then add in the bouillon and evenly mix it in.
5. Once the bouillon has been added.
6. Combine in the red pepper and the rest of the oil.
7. Keep cooking the mix for 12 more mins then stir in the cheese, sausage, and pasta.
8. Let everything get hot for 7 mins.
9. Enjoy.

Ginger Garlic
Basmati with Squash

Prep Time: 10 mins
Total Time: 30 mins

Servings per Recipe: 8	
Calories	247.5
Fat	9.0g
Cholesterol	20.3mg
Sodium	390.9mg
Carbohydrates	39.0g
Protein	4.2g

Ingredients

1 lb. butternut squash, peeled, seeded and cut into cubes
2 C. minced onions
3 tbsp minced ginger
1 tbsp minced garlic
1/3 C. butter
1 1/2 C. basmati rice, rinsed and drained
1 1/2 tbsp curry powder
1/2 tsp salt
3 C. de-fatted chicken broth

2 tbsp chopped cilantro

Directions

1. In a 5-6-quart pan, melt the butter over medium heat and cook onions, garlic and ginger for about 10-15 minutes, stirring frequently.
2. Add the rice and cook for about 5 minutes, stirring occasionally.
3. Add the curry powder and cook for about 30 seconds, stirring continuously.
4. Stir in the squash, broth and 1/2 tsp of the salt and bring to a boil over high heat.
5. Reduce the heat to low and simmer, covered for about 16-18 minutes, stirring occasionally.
6. Stir in the cilantro and salt and serve.

GINGER, TOMATO, and Coconut Potato Skillet

Prep Time: 15 mins
Total Time: 50 mins

Servings per Recipe: 4

Calories	372 kcal
Fat	26.8 g
Carbohydrates	32.2g
Protein	6.2 g
Cholesterol	0 mg
Sodium	66 mg

Ingredients

1 tablespoon olive oil
1 pound small potatoes, halved
2 red onions, chopped
5 cloves garlic, minced
1 (1 inch) piece fresh ginger root, minced
1 teaspoon ground turmeric
1 tablespoon cumin seeds

salt and pepper to taste
1 (16 ounce) can coconut milk
2 tablespoons tomato puree
1 bunch fresh parsley, chopped

Directions

1. Get your olive oil hot in a frying pan then once the oil is hot begin to fry your potatoes in the oil for 12 until the potatoes are completely golden then place them to the side.
2. Now begin to fry your onions for 3 mins then combine in the pepper, garlic, salt, ginger, cumin seeds, and turmeric.
3. Let the spices and onions cook for 60 secs then add the potatoes back let everything fry for 17 mins.
4. Add in your coconut milk and the tomato puree and stir then combine in the parsley and stir again. Let everything cook for 7 more mins.
5. Enjoy.

Los Angeles Lunch

🥣 Prep Time: 25 mins

🕐 Total Time: 25 mins

Servings per Recipe: 8	
Calories	321 kcal
Fat	28.7 g
Carbohydrates	13.5g
Protein	4.9 g
Cholesterol	16 mg
Sodium	419 mg

Ingredients

1 avocado, peeled and pitted
1 tbsp lemon juice
1/2 C. mayonnaise
1/4 tsp hot pepper sauce
1/4 C. olive oil
1 clove garlic, peeled and minced
1/2 tsp salt
1 head romaine lettuce- rinsed, dried and torn into bite sized pieces
3 oz. Cheddar cheese, shredded

2 tomatoes, diced
2 green onions, chopped
1/4 (2.25 oz.) can pitted green olives
1 C. coarsely crushed corn chips

Directions

1. In a food processor, add avocado, garlic, mayonnaise, hot pepper sauce, olive oil, lemon juice and salt and pulse till smooth.
2. In a large bowl, mix together the romaine lettuce, tomatoes, olives, green onions, Cheddar cheese and corn chips.
3. Pour dressing over and toss to coat well.
4. Serve immediately.

GOURMET
Lunch

Prep Time: 15 mins
Total Time: 20 mins

Servings per Recipe: 4	
Calories	663 kcal
Fat	40.6 g
Carbohydrates	40.1g
Protein	36.1 g
Cholesterol	293 mg
Sodium	1085 mg

Ingredients

1 (10 oz.) bag baby spinach leaves
4 hard-cooked eggs, peeled and sliced
1 C. sliced mushrooms
4 strips crisply cooked bacon, crumbled
10 oz. Swiss cheese, shredded
1/2 C. toasted sliced almonds
1 tbsp olive oil
1 large shallot, minced
1 tsp garlic, minced
1/3 C. white wine vinegar

1/3 C. Dijon mustard
1/3 C. honey
2 strips crisply cooked bacon, crumbled
salt and pepper to taste

Directions

1. In a large bowl, place the spinach, eggs, mushrooms, 4 crumbled bacon strips, Swiss cheese and almonds.

2. In a small skillet, heat the olive oil on medium heat and sauté the shallots and garlic for about 2 minutes.

3. Stir in the vinegar, honey, Dijon mustard, 2 crumbled bacon strips, salt and pepper and cook till heated completely.

4. Pour hot dressing over the spinach mixture and toss to coat well.

5. Serve immediately.

Texas
Sirloin Salad

🥣 Prep Time: 30 mins

🕐 Total Time: 45 mins

Servings per Recipe: 5	
Calories	496 kcal
Fat	36.4 g
Carbohydrates	10.1g
Protein	32.6 g
Cholesterol	100 mg
Sodium	836 mg

Ingredients

1 3/4 lb. beef sirloin steak
1/3 C. olive oil
3 tbsp red wine vinegar
2 tbsp lemon juice
1 clove garlic, minced
1/2 tsp salt
1/8 tsp ground black pepper
1 tsp Worcestershire sauce
3/4 C. crumbled blue cheese
8 C. romaine lettuce - rinsed, dried, and

torn into bite-size pieces
2 tomatoes, sliced
1 small green bell pepper, sliced
1 carrot, sliced
1/2 C. sliced red onion
1/4 C. sliced pimento-stuffed green olives

Directions

1. In a small bowl, add the garlic, vinegar, lemon juice, oil, salt and black pepper and beat till well combined.
2. Add the cheese and stir to combine.
3. Refrigerate to chill before serving.
4. Set your grill for high heat and lightly, grease the grill grate.
5. Cook the steak on the grill for about 3-5 minutes per side.
6. Remove from the grill and place the steak onto a cutting board for about 5 minutes before slicing.
7. Cut the steak into bite size pieces.
8. Arrange the lettuce, onto chilled plates, followed by the tomato, pepper, onion, olives and steak pieces.
9. Drizzle with the dressing and serve.

HOW TO MAKE
a Caesar Salad

🥣 Prep Time: 20 mins
🕐 Total Time: 1 hr 25 mins

Servings per Recipe: 5

Calories	544 kcal
Fat	44.2 g
Carbohydrates	25.4g
Protein	11.5 g
Cholesterol	48 mg
Sodium	992 mg

Ingredients

1 head romaine lettuce
3/4 C. extra virgin olive oil
3 tbsp red wine vinegar
1 tsp Worcestershire sauce
1/2 tsp salt
1/4 tbsp ground mustard
1 clove crushed garlic
1 egg
1 lemon, juiced
freshly ground black pepper

1/4 C. grated Parmesan cheese
1 1/2 C. garlic croutons
1 (2 oz.) can anchovy filets

Directions

1. Clean the lettuce completely and with paper towels, absorb the moisture.
2. Refrigerate for at least 1 hour before using.
3. In a bowl, add the garlic, lemon juice, vinegar, oil, Worcestershire sauce, mustard and salt and beat till well combined.
4. In a pan, add 3 C. of the water and bring to a boil.
5. Drop in egg with shell for about 1 minute.
6. Remove the egg from water and keep aside to cool.
7. After cooling, crack the egg into dressing and beat till well combined.
8. In a small bowl, add thee desired amount of anchovies and mash them.
9. Add the mashed anchovies into the dressing and mix well.
10. In a large bowl, place torn lettuce leaves and dressing and gently, toss to coat.
11. Add the remaining ingredients and toss to coat well.
12. Serve immediately.

Multi-colored
Pepperoni Pasta Salad with Oregano Dressing

🥣 Prep Time: 35 mins

🕐 Total Time: 8 hrs 45 mins

Servings per Recipe: 8	
Calories	443 kcal
Fat	32 g
Carbohydrates	25.4g
Protein	15.9 g
Cholesterol	39 mg
Sodium	836 mg

Ingredients

1 (8 oz) package uncooked tri-color Rotini pasta
6 oz pepperoni sausage, diced
6 oz provolone cheese, cubed
1 red onion, thinly sliced
1 small cucumber, thinly sliced
3/4 C. chopped green bell pepper
3/4 C. chopped red bell pepper
1 (6 oz) can pitted black olives
1/4 C. minced fresh parsley
1/4 C. grated Parmesan cheese
1/2 C. olive oil

1/4 C. red wine vinegar
2 cloves garlic, minced
1 tsp dried basil
1 tsp dried oregano
1/2 tsp ground mustard seed
1/4 tsp salt
1/8 tsp ground black pepper

Directions

1. Cook the pasta according to the directions on the package.
2. Get a small jar or a small mixing bowl: Combine in it the olive oil, vinegar, garlic, basil, oregano, ground mustard, salt, and pepper. Mix them well to make the dressing.
3. Get a large mixing bowl: Toss in it the dressing with the remaining ingredients. Place the salad in the fridge for an overnight.
4. Adjust the seasoning of the salad then serve it.
5. Enjoy.

SOUTHERN
Honey and Dijon Collard Green Salad

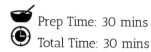

Prep Time: 30 mins
Total Time: 30 mins

Servings per Recipe: 4
Calories	421 kcal
Fat	27.8 g
Carbohydrates	43.8g
Protein	7.5 g
Cholesterol	0 mg
Sodium	394 mg

Ingredients

Salad:
4 collard leaves, trimmed and finely chopped
1/3 bunch kale, trimmed and chopped
1 head romaine lettuce, chopped
1/4 small head red cabbage, chopped
1 Bosc pear, cubed
1/2 Bermuda onion, finely diced
1/2 orange bell pepper, diced
1/2 Florida avocado - peeled, pitted, and diced
1/2 carrot, grated
5 cherry tomatoes, halved
7 walnut halves, crushed
2 tbsp raisins

Dressing:
6 tbsp olive oil
3 tbsp balsamic vinegar
1 tbsp wildflower honey
1 tbsp oregano, crushed
1 1/2 tsp chili powder
1 tsp Dijon mustard
1 clove garlic, minced
1/2 tsp salt
1/4 tsp crushed black peppercorns

Directions

1. In a large bowl, mix together all salad ingredients.
2. In a jar, add all dressing ingredients.
3. Seal the jar and shake well to combine.
4. Pour the dressing over salad and toss to coat well.
5. Serve immediately.

Farfalle
Lemon Salad

🥣 Prep Time: 10 mins

🕐 Total Time: 2 hrs 25 mins

Servings per Recipe: 8	
Calories	334 kcal
Fat	16.6 g
Carbohydrates	41.8g
Protein	8.6 g
Cholesterol	6 mg
Sodium	1167 mg

Ingredients

1 (12 oz) package Farfalle pasta
10 oz baby spinach, rinsed and torn into bite-size piece
2 oz crumbled feta cheese with basil and tomato
1 red onion, chopped
1 (15 oz) can black olives, drained and chopped
1 C. Italian-style salad dressing
4 cloves garlic, minced

1 lemon, juiced
1/2 tsp garlic salt
1/2 tsp ground black pepper

Directions

1. Cook the pasta according to the directions on the package.
2. Get a small mixing bowl: Combine in it the salad dressing, garlic, lemon juice, garlic salt and pepper. Mix them well to make the dressing.
3. Get a large mixing bowl: Combine in it the pasta, spinach, cheese, red onion and olives. Add the dressing and toss them well.
4. Place the salad in the fridge for 3 h to an overnight then serve it.
5. Enjoy.

GREEK STYLE
Chicken Pasta Salad

Prep Time: 45 mins
Total Time: 53 mins

Servings per Recipe: 6
Calories	425 kcal
Fat	18.9 g
Carbohydrates	44.7g
Protein	21.8 g
Cholesterol	35 mg
Sodium	358 mg

Ingredients

1 tsp finely chopped, peeled fresh ginger
1/3 C. rice vinegar
1/4 C. orange juice
1/4 C. vegetable oil
1 tsp toasted sesame oil
1 (1 oz) package dry onion soup mix
2 tsp white sugar
1 clove garlic, pressed
1 (8 oz) package bow tie (farfalle) pasta
1/2 cucumber - scored, halved lengthwise, seeded, and sliced
1/2 C. diced red bell pepper
1/2 C. coarsely chopped red onion
2 diced Roma tomatoes

1 carrot, shredded
1 (6 oz) bag fresh spinach
1 (11 oz) can mandarin orange segments, drained
2 C. diced cooked chicken
1/2 C. sliced almonds, toasted

Directions

1. Get a small mixing bowl: Combine in it the ginger root, rice vinegar, orange juice, vegetable oil, sesame oil, soup mix, sugar, and garlic.
2. Mix them well to make the dressing. Place it in the fridge.
3. Cook the pasta according to the directions on the package.
4. Get a large mixing bowl: Combine in it all the ingredients. Drizzle the dressing on top and toss the salad to coat. Adjust the seasoning of the salad and serve it.
5. Enjoy.

Prosciutto Pasta Salad

🥣 Prep Time: 15 mins

🕐 Total Time: 30 mins

Servings per Recipe: 10	
Calories	372 kcal
Fat	20.7 g
Carbohydrates	36.4g
Protein	13.6 g
Cholesterol	15 mg
Sodium	329 mg

Ingredients

1 (16 oz) package bow tie pasta
1 (6 oz) package spinach leaves
2 C. fresh basil leaves
1/2 C. extra virgin olive oil
3 cloves garlic, minced
4 oz prosciutto, diced

salt and ground black pepper to taste
3/4 C. freshly grated Parmesan cheese
1/2 C. toasted pine nuts

Directions

1. Cook the pasta according to the directions on the package.
2. Place a large pan over medium heat. Heat the oil in it. Add the garlic and cook it for 60 sec. Add the prosciutto and cook them for 4 min.
3. Get a large mixing bowl: Transfer the prosciutto and garlic mix to the mixing bowl with the pasta, spinach, basil, a pinch of salt and pepper. Toss them well.
4. Top your pasta with pine nuts and parmesan. Serve it.
5. Enjoy.

FRUITY
Salmon Macaroni Salad with Yogurt Dressing

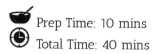

Prep Time: 10 mins
Total Time: 40 mins

Servings per Recipe: 8
Calories	222 kcal
Fat	12.3 g
Carbohydrates	17.6 g
Protein	11 g
Cholesterol	18 mg
Sodium	208 mg

Ingredients

1 C. dry pasta, such as macaroni or small shells
8 oz cooked, skinned salmon
1/2 C. minced red or yellow onion
1 C. diced celery
1 medium red apple, diced
1/2 C. chopped walnuts or dry-roasted, unsalted peanuts
Dressing:
1 (6 oz) container fat-free yogurt

2 tbsp olive oil
1 tbsp curry powder
2 tsp fresh lemon juice
2 cloves garlic, crushed
1 tsp Dijon mustard
1/2 tsp salt (or to taste)
Freshly ground black pepper, to taste

Directions

1. Cook the pasta according to the directions on the package.
2. Get a small mixing bowl: Combine in it the dressing ingredients. Mix them well.
3. Get a large mixing bowl: Combine in it the salad ingredients. Add the dressing and stir them well.
4. Adjust the seasoning of the salad. Place it in the fridge until ready to serve.
5. Enjoy.

Vegan
Rigatoni Basil Salad

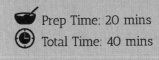 Prep Time: 20 mins

Total Time: 40 mins

Servings per Recipe: 6

Calories	387 kcal
Fat	16.7 g
Carbohydrates	47.8g
Protein	11.9 g
Cholesterol	0 mg
Sodium	89 mg

Ingredients

1 1/2 (8 oz) packages rigatoni pasta
2 tbsp olive oil
2 cloves garlic, minced
1/2 (16 oz) package tofu, drained and cubed
1/2 tsp dried thyme
1 1/2 tsp soy sauce
1 small onion, thinly sliced

1 large tomato, cubed
1 carrot, shredded
6 leaves fresh basil, thinly sliced
6 sprigs fresh cilantro, minced
1/4 C. olive oil

Directions

1. Cook the pasta according to the directions on the package.
2. Place a large pan over medium heat. Heat 2 tbsp of olive oil in it. Add the garlic and cook it for 1 min 30 sec.
3. Stir in the thyme with tofu. Cook them for 9 min. Stir in the soy sauce and turn off the heat.
4. Get a large mixing bowl: Toss in it the rigatoni, tofu mix, onion, tomato, carrot, basil, and cilantro. Drizzle the olive oil over the pasta salad then serve it.
5. Enjoy.

MINTY
Feta and Orzo Salad

Prep Time: 30 mins
Total Time: 2 hrs 50 mins

Servings per Recipe: 8
Calories	374 kcal
Fat	19 g
Carbohydrates	38.2g
Protein	13.3 g
Cholesterol	25 mg
Sodium	456 mg

Ingredients

1 1/4 C. orzo pasta
6 tbsp olive oil, divided
3/4 C. dried brown lentils, rinsed and drained
1/3 C. red wine vinegar
3 cloves garlic, minced
1/2 C. kalamata olives, pitted and chopped
1 1/2 C. crumbled feta cheese
1 small red onion, diced

1/2 C. finely chopped fresh mint leaves
1/2 C. chopped fresh dill
salt and pepper to taste

Directions

1. Cook the pasta according to the directions on the package.
2. Bring a salted large saucepan of water to a boil. Cook in it the lentils until it starts boiling.
3. Lower the heat and put on the lid. Cook the lentils for 22 min. Remove them from the water.
4. Get a small mixing bowl: Combine in it the olive oil, vinegar, and garlic. Whisk them well to make the dressing.
5. Get a large mixing bowl: Toss in it the lentils, dressing, olives, feta cheese, red onion, mint, and dill, with salt and pepper.
6. Wrap a plastic wrap on the salad bowl and place it in the fridge for 2 h 30 min. Adjust the seasoning of the salad then serve it.
7. Enjoy.

Herbed
Feta and Roasted Turkey Salad

🥣 Prep Time: 30 mins
🕐 Total Time: 30 mins

Servings per Recipe: 8	
Calories	767 kcal
Fat	65.3 g
Carbohydrates	24.6g
Protein	21.4 g
Cholesterol	59 mg
Sodium	1270 mg

Ingredients

1 1/2 C. olive oil
1/2 C. red wine vinegar
1 tbsp minced fresh garlic
2 tsp dried oregano leaves
3 C. Butterball(R) Golden Oven Roasted
Turkey Breast, sliced thick and cubed
3 C. cooked penne pasta
1 (16 oz) jar pitted kalamata olives,
drained, chopped
1 pint grape tomatoes, halved
8 oz crumbled feta cheese
1 (5 oz) package spring lettuce mix
1/2 C. chopped Italian parsley
1/2 C. thinly sliced red onions

Directions

1. Get a small mixing bowl: Combine in it the olive oil, vinegar, garlic and oregano. Mix them well to make the vinaigrette.
2. Get a large mixing bowl: Toss in it the rest of ingredients. Add the dressing and mix them again. Adjust the seasoning of the salad then serve it.
3. Enjoy.

NUTTY
Tuna and Pasta Salad

 Prep Time: 25 mins

Total Time: 45 mins

Servings per Recipe: 6

Calories	906 kcal
Fat	49.3 g
Carbohydrates	66.9g
Protein	50.8 g
Cholesterol	85 mg
Sodium	672 mg

Ingredients

1 head broccoli, separated into florets
1 lb penne pasta
1 lb fresh tuna steaks
1/4 C. water
2 tbsp fresh lemon juice
1/4 C. white wine
4 medium tomatoes, quartered
1 lb mozzarella cheese, diced
8 large black olives, sliced
1/2 C. walnut pieces, toasted

4 cloves garlic, minced
2 tbsp chopped fresh parsley
4 anchovy fillets, rinsed
3/4 C. olive oil

Directions

1. Cook the pasta according to the directions on the package.
2. Bring a salted pot of water to a boil. Cook in it the broccoli for 5 min. Remove it from the water and place it aside.
3. Place a large pan over medium heat. Stir in it the tuna in a with water, white wine, and lemon juice. put on the lid and cook them until the salmon is done for about 8 to 12 min.
4. Bread the salmon fillets into chunks.
5. Get a large mixing bowl: Toss in it the cooked salmon fish with broccoli, penne, fish, tomatoes, cheese, olives, walnuts, garlic, and parsley. Mix them well.
6. Place a large skillet over medium heat. Heat the oil in it. Slice the anchovies into small pieces. Cook them in the heated skillet until they melt in the oil.
7. Stir the mix into the pasta salad and mix them well. Serve your pasta salad right away.
8. Enjoy.

Roasted Kalamata Rotini Salad

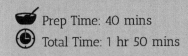

Prep Time: 40 mins
Total Time: 1 hr 50 mins

Servings per Recipe: 10	
Calories	478 kcal
Fat	34.7 g
Carbohydrates	39.9g
Protein	8.4 g
Cholesterol	0 mg
Sodium	1614 mg

Ingredients

1 (12 oz) package tri-colored rotini pasta
1 small head broccoli, broken into small florets
1/2 tsp minced garlic
1 small red onion, diced
1 (12 oz) jar marinated artichoke hearts, drained and chopped
1 (12 oz) jar pitted kalamata olives, sliced
1 (8 oz) jar roasted red bell peppers, drained, cut into strips

4 Roma tomatoes, diced
1 (12 oz) jar oil-packed sun-dried tomatoes, drained, cut into strips
1 small zucchini, chopped
1 small cucumber, chopped
1 small yellow bell pepper, chopped
2 ripe avocados
1 (16 oz) bottle Greek vinaigrette salad dressing

Directions

1. Cook the pasta according to the directions on the package.
2. Bring a large pot of water to a boil. Place a steamer on it. Cook in it the broccoli for 5 min with the lid on.
3. Clean the broccoli with some cool water and drain it. Chop it and place it aside.
4. Get a large mixing bowl: Combine in it the broccoli with pasta, garlic, red onion, artichoke hearts, kalamata olives, roasted red peppers, Roma tomatoes, sun-dried tomatoes, zucchini, cucumber, and yellow pepper.
5. Mix them well.
6. Get a small mixing bowl: Mash in it the avocado until it becomes smooth. Add the Greek dressing and mix them well until they become creamy to make the dressing.
7. Add the avocado dressing to the salad and toss it well. Adjust the seasoning of the salad and chill it in the fridge until ready to serve.
8. Enjoy.

NUTTY
Farfalle Salad with Dijon Dressing

Prep Time: 15 mins
Total Time: 1 hr 30 mins

Servings per Recipe: 8
Calories	505 kcal
Fat	26.7 g
Carbohydrates	50.7g
Protein	18.9 g
Cholesterol	20 mg
Sodium	731 mg

Ingredients

1 1/2 tbsp white sugar
1 tsp salt, or to taste
1 1/2 tsp ground black pepper
1 tsp onion powder
1 1/2 tsp Dijon mustard
2 cloves garlic, chopped
1 1/2 C. chopped fresh basil
1/2 C. chopped fresh oregano
1/4 C. chopped fresh cilantro
2 tsp hot pepper sauce
1/3 C. red wine vinegar
1/2 C. olive oil

1 tsp lemon juice
1 (4 oz) package grated Parmesan cheese
4 roma (plum) tomatoes, chopped
6 green onions, chopped
1 (4 oz) can minced black olives
1 (16 oz) package farfalle (bow tie) pasta
1/2 C. pine nuts
1 C. shredded mozzarella cheese

Directions

1. Get a large mixing bowl: Combine in it the sugar, salt, pepper, onion powder, mustard, garlic, basil, oregano, cilantro, hot pepper sauce, red wine vinegar, olive oil, lemon juice, and Parmesan cheese.
2. Mix them well. Stir in the tomatoes, green onions and olives. Mix them again. Place the mix in the fridge.
3. Cook the pasta according to the directions on the package.
4. Stir the pasta into the salad bowl and mix them well. Top your salad with mozzarella cheese and pine nuts. Chill it in the fridge until ready to serve.
5. Enjoy.

Tomato
Parmesan Spinach

🥣 Prep Time: 15 mins

🕐 Total Time: 45 mins

Servings per Recipe: 10	
Calories	423 kcal
Carbohydrates	39 g
Cholesterol	89 mg
Fat	19.3 g
Protein	22.3 g
Sodium	1077 mg

Ingredients

3/4 lb pasta
1 tbsp olive oil
1 lb spicy Italian sausage
1 onion, chopped
4 cloves garlic, diced
1 (14.5 oz) can chicken broth
1 tsp dried basil

1 (14.5 oz) can diced tomatoes
1 (10 oz) package frozen chopped spinach
1/2 C. grated Parmesan cheese

Directions

1. For 8 mins boil pasta in water and salt until al dente. Remove excess water.
2. Get a frying pan. Stir fry your garlic and onions in oil. Then for 5 mins fry your sausage until fully cooked. Mix in your basil, tomatoes (with sauce), and broth.
3. Add your spinach then lightly boil for 6 mins or spinach becomes soft.
4. Combine pasta and sausage cook for 2 mins. Then garnish with cheese.
5. Enjoy.

PASTA
Tomato Soup

Prep Time: 10 mins
Total Time: 50 mins

Servings per Recipe: 4
Calories	225 kcal
Carbohydrates	37.3 g
Cholesterol	2 mg
Fat	4.4 g
Protein	11 g
Sodium	758 mg

Ingredients

1 tbsp olive oil
2 stalks celery, chopped
1 onion, chopped
3 cloves garlic, diced
2 tsps dried parsley
1 tsp Italian seasoning
1/4 tsp mashed red pepper flakes
salt to taste
1 (14.5 oz) can chicken broth

2 medium tomatoes, peeled and chopped
1 (8 oz) can tomato sauce
1/2 C. uncooked spinach pasta
1 (15 oz) can cannellini beans, with liquid

Directions

1. Stir fry your salt, celery, red pepper flakes, onions, Italian seasoning, parsley, and garlic in olive oil for 6 mins.
2. Combine in tomato sauce, broth, and tomatoes. Bring everything to a light boil over medium to low heat and cook for 17 mins.
3. Mix in your pasta and continue cooking for 12 more mins until pasta is soft.
4. Finally combine in your beans with sauce, and heat them up. Garnish everything with some parmesan.
5. Enjoy.

Shrimp
Penne

Prep Time: 10 mins
Total Time: 40 mins

Servings per Recipe: 4
Calories   411 kcal
Carbohydrates   50.4 g
Cholesterol   0 mg
Fat   9.3 g
Protein   24 g
Sodium   313 mg

Ingredients

6 oz penne pasta
1 onion, chopped
2 tbsps olive oil
1 clove garlic, diced
1 green bell pepper, sliced
3 stalks celery, chopped
1 (14.5 oz) can diced tomatoes

1 1/2 C. dry hard cider
1 1/2 tbsps tomato paste
salt to taste
ground black pepper to taste
3/4 lb fresh prawns

Directions

1. Fry your onions for 4 mins in olive oil. Then add the following: celery, garlic, and bell pepper. Fry for 6 more mins.
2. Combine with the onions: salt, tomatoes, pepper, tomato puree, and dry cider. Get it boiling.
3. Once boiling combine in your pasta. Place a lid on the pan. Lightly boil for 20 mins.
4. Add your prawns to everything and continue simmering for 6 more mins.
5. Enjoy.

CANNELLINI
Classic

🥣 Prep Time: 10 mins
🕐 Total Time: 50 mins

Servings per Recipe: 6	
Calories	452 kcal
Carbohydrates	59.3 g
Cholesterol	16 mg
Fat	17.7 g
Protein	15.7 g
Sodium	228 mg

Ingredients

3 cloves garlic, diced
1 onion, chopped
1 carrot, finely chopped
2 tbsps chopped fresh parsley
2 tsps dried basil
1 tsp dried oregano
4 tbsps olive oil
1 (14.5 oz) can whole peeled tomatoes
2 C. cooked cannellini beans, drained
and rinsed

8 oz macaroni
2 tbsps butter
1/4 C. grated Parmesan cheese
salt and pepper to taste

Directions

1. Stir fry, in olive oil, until onions are soft: onions, basil, carrots, garlic, parsley, and oregano. Mix in some salt and pepper, tomatoes, and 1/4 C. of tomato juice. Cook for 12 mins.
2. Combine in the cannellini and place a lid on the pan. Simmer for 20 mins with lower heat.
3. Boil your macaroni in salt and water until al dente about 10 to 12 mins. Then coat with butter and parmesan. Mix the coated noodles with the cannellini and enjoy.

Cajun Style Penne

🥣 Prep Time: 15 mins
🕐 Total Time: 45 mins

Servings per Recipe: 8
Calories	457 kcal
Carbohydrates	68 g
Cholesterol	45 mg
Fat	9.6 g
Protein	24.7 g
Sodium	1107 mg

Ingredients

1 lb penne pasta
2 tbsps butter, divided
4 boneless, skinless chicken breasts, trimmed of fat and cut crosswise into 1/4-inch slices
2 tbsps Cajun-style blackened seasoning
4 cloves garlic, chopped
1 large red onion, cut into wedges
1 green bell pepper, seeded and sliced into strips

1 red bell pepper, seeded and sliced into strips
1 yellow bell pepper, seeded and sliced into strips
1 tsp mashed red pepper flakes
1/4 tsp curry powder
salt and pepper to taste
2 (24 oz) jars meatless spaghetti sauce

Directions

1. Boil pasta in salt and water for 10 mins. Drain excess liquid. Set aside.
2. Get a frying pan and stir fry your chicken in 1 tbsp of butter until fully done and brown. Remove chicken from the pan.
3. Fry onions, salt and pepper, garlic, curry powder, all the julienned peppers, and red pepper flakes until the onions have browned and everything is soft. Mix back in your chicken and the tomato sauce.
4. Heat for 3 mins. Let the flavors settle for 5 mins.
5. Enjoy.

FRESH SEASONING
Pasta

Prep Time: 15 mins
Total Time: 30 mins

Servings per Recipe: 4
Calories	379 kcal
Carbohydrates	32.9 g
Cholesterol	102 mg
Fat	24.8 g
Protein	7.1 g
Sodium	216 mg

Ingredients

1/2 lb uncooked pasta
1/2 C. butter
4 cloves garlic, diced
3 tbsps chopped fresh basil
1 tbsp chopped fresh thyme
1 tsp dried marjoram
1 tsp ground savory
1 tbsp chopped fresh parsley

salt to taste
ground black pepper to taste
2 tbsps sliced black olives

Directions

1. Boil pasta in salt and water for 10 mins. Remove liquid and set aside.
2. Get a frying pan and melt some butter, and all the seasonings. Cook for 3 mins to flavor your butter.
3. Coat your pasta with the flavored butter. Add some salt and pepper, and garnish with olives.
4. Enjoy.

Plantain
Steak Sandwich

🍳 Prep Time: 10 mins
🕐 Total Time: 25 mins

Servings per Recipe: 1
Calories	1219 kcal
Fat	100.4 g
Carbohydrates	65.4g
Protein	23.6 g
Cholesterol	68 mg
Sodium	551 mg

Ingredients

2 C. vegetable oil for frying
1 green plantain, peeled and halved lengthwise
2 tbsp vegetable oil
1 clove garlic, minced
4 oz beef skirt steak, cut into thin strips
1/4 medium yellow onion, thinly sliced
1 pinch cumin
1 pinch dried oregano
1 tbsp mayonnaise

1 slice processed American cheese, cut in half
2 slices tomato
3 leaves lettuce

Directions

1. Place a large pan over medium heat. Heat 2 C. of oil in it. Cook in it the plantains for 2 to 3 min or until they become golden.
2. Drain the plantains and place them on a board. Use a rolling pin or the back of a skillet to flatten them.
3. Place them back in the hot oil and cook them for another 3 min and become golden brown. Drain them and place them aside.
4. Place a large pan over medium heat. Heat in it 2 tbsp of oil. Sauté in it the garlic, skirt steak, onion, cumin and oregano for 8 min while stirring often.
5. Use a knife to spread the mayo over the fried plantains and place one of them on a serving plate.
6. Lay over it the cheese with steak mixture, lettuce, and tomato. Cover them with the second half of the plantain then serve it.
7. Enjoy.

SPICY GARBANZO
and Turkey Stew

Prep Time: 15 mins
Total Time: 5 hrs 15 mins

Servings per Recipe: 6
Calories	238.3
Fat	1.5g
Cholesterol	70.3mg
Sodium	850.1mg
Carbohydrates	22.0g
Protein	34.3g

Ingredients

1 1/2 lbs turkey tenderloins, cut into
3/4 inch pieces
1 tbsp chili powder
1 tsp ground cumin
3/4 tsp salt
1 (15 oz) cans diced tomatoes with mild
green chilies
1 (15 oz) cans garbanzo beans, drained
and rinsed (optional)
1 (15 oz) cans black beans, drained but
not rinsed
1 (15 1/2 oz) cans pinto beans in chili
sauce, un-drained

1 (4 oz) cans mild green chilies (optional)
1 red bell pepper, cut into 3/4 inch
pieces
1 green bell pepper, cut into 3/4 inch
pieces
3/4 C. onion, chopped
3/4 C. salsa
3 garlic cloves, minced
fresh cilantro (optional)

Directions

1. Combine the turkey tenderloins with chili powder, cumin and salt in a greased slow cooker.
2. Stir into them the beans, tomatoes, chilies, bell peppers, onion, salsa and garlic.
3. Put on the lid and let them cook for 6 h on low.
4. Once the time is up, serve your stew hot.
5. Enjoy.

Chicago City
Chili

🥣 Prep Time: 15 mins
🕐 Total Time: 4 hrs 15 mins

Servings per Recipe: 10
Calories	389 kcal
Fat	11.5 g
Carbohydrates	41.4g
Protein	26.3 g
Cholesterol	55 mg
Sodium	890 mg

Ingredients

2 lbs ground beef
4 (14.5 ounce) cans kidney beans
4 (15 ounce) cans diced tomatoes
1 (12 ounce) bottle tomato-based chili sauce
1 large white onion, chopped
6 cloves garlic, minced
2 tbsps chili seasoning
1 tsp black pepper
1/2 tsp garlic powder

1/2 tsp onion powder
1/2 tsp cayenne pepper
1/2 tsp oregano
1/4 C. sugar
1 tsp hot sauce
1 tsp Worcestershire sauce

Directions

1. Place a Dutch oven over medium heat. Cook in it the beef for 8 min. discard the excess fat.
2. Stir in the remaining ingredients. Cook them until they start boiling. Lower the heat and put on the lid.
3. Cook the stew for 4 h while stirring every once in a while then serve it warm.
4. Enjoy.

COMFORTING
Quinoa Lunch

Prep Time: 30 mins
Total Time: 1 hr

Servings per Recipe: 10
Calories	233 kcal
Fat	3.5 g
Carbohydrates	42g
Protein	11.5 g
Cholesterol	0 mg
Sodium	540 mg

Ingredients

1 C. uncooked quinoa, rinsed
2 C. water
1 tbsp vegetable oil
1 onion, diced
4 cloves garlic, diced
1 tbsp chili powder
1 tbsp ground cumin
1 (28 oz.) can crushed tomatoes
2 (19 oz.) cans black beans, rinsed and drained
1 green bell pepper, diced

1 red bell pepper, diced
1 zucchini, diced
1 jalapeno pepper, seeded and minced
1 tbsp minced chipotle peppers in adobo sauce
1 tsp dried oregano
salt and ground black pepper to taste
1 C. frozen corn
1/4 C. diced fresh cilantro

Directions

1. Boil your quinoa in water for 2 mins before placing a lid on the pot, setting the heat to low, and letting the quinoa cook for 17 mins.
2. Stir the quinoa once it has cooled off.
3. At the same time, stir fry the onions for 7 mins, in veggie oil, and then add in the cumin, garlic, and chili powder.
4. Cook this mix for 2 more mins then add: oregano, tomatoes, chipotles, beans, jalapenos, bell peppers, and zucchini.
5. Stir the contents before adding your preferred amount of pepper and salt.
6. Get everything boiling and then place a lid on the pot.
7. Let the contents gently boil over low heat for 22 mins then add in the corn and quinoa.
8. Continue simmering for 7 more mins before adding cilantro.
9. Enjoy.

Vegetarian Fajitas

Prep Time: 15 mins
Total Time: 25 mins

Servings per Recipe: 5	
Calories	424 kcal
Fat	11.3 g
Carbohydrates	67.4g
Protein	29.7 g
Cholesterol	0 mg
Sodium	924 mg

Ingredients

3 tbsp olive oil
1 red bell pepper, cut into strips
1 green bell pepper, cut into strips
1 yellow bell pepper, cut into strips
1/2 red onion, chopped
1 lb. seitan, cut into strips
2 tbsp reduced-soy sauce
3 cloves garlic, minced
1 tsp chili powder

1 tsp paprika
1 tsp ground cumin
10 whole grain tortillas

Directions

1. In a large skillet, heat the oil on medium heat and sauté the red bell pepper, green bell pepper, yellow bell pepper and onion for about 3-5 minutes.
2. Add the seitan, soy sauce, garlic, chili powder, paprika and cumin and cook for about 7-10 minutes.
3. Place the seitan filling onto each tortilla and fold the tortilla around filling.

BARBEQUE PARTY
Fajitas

Prep Time: 20 mins
Total Time: 1 hr

Servings per Recipe: 6

Calories	248 kcal
Fat	16 g
Carbohydrates	5g
Protein	20.4 g
Cholesterol	49 mg
Sodium	44 mg

Ingredients

Marinade:
1/4 C. extra-virgin olive oil
1/2 lime, zested and juiced
2 cloves garlic, minced
1/2 tsp ground cumin
1/4 tsp red pepper flakes
1/4 tsp ground chipotle pepper
1 1/2 lb. beef sirloin, cut into 1-inch cubes
1 red bell pepper, cut into 1-inch cubes

1 green bell pepper, cut into 1-inch cubes
1/2 onion, cut into 1-inch cubes
skewers

Directions

1. In a large glass bowl, add the olive oil, lime juice, lime zest, garlic, cumin, red pepper flakes and chipotle pepper and beat till well combined.
2. Add the sirloin and toss to coat evenly.
3. With a plastic wrap, cover the bowl and refrigerate to marinate for about 30 minutes to 2 hours.
4. Set your outdoor grill for medium-high heat and lightly grease the grill grate.
5. Remove sirloin from the marinade and discard the excess marinade.
6. Thread the sirloin, red bell pepper, green bell pepper and onion onto skewers.
7. Cook on the grill until sirloin for about 4 minutes per side.

Easy Japanese
Grill Fried Rice

🥣 Prep Time: 10 mins
🕐 Total Time: 20 mins

Servings per Recipe: 6	
Calories	226 kcal
Fat	12.6 g
Carbohydrates	17.1g
Protein	10.7 g
Cholesterol	80 mg
Sodium	491 mg

Ingredients

1/4 C. olive oil
2 eggs, beaten
1 C. chopped grilled chicken
1/2 C. chopped green onion
2 tbsp chopped garlic

2 C. cooked white rice
3 tbsp soy sauce

Directions

1. In a large non-stick skillet, heat the olive oil on medium-high heat and cook the eggs for about 2-3 minutes, stirring continuously.
2. Stir in the chicken, green onion and garlic and cook for about 2 minutes.
3. Stir in the rice and cook for about 2 minutes.
4. Stir in the soy sauce and cook for about 3 minutes.

SUN BELT
Bison Fajitas

Prep Time: 30 mins
Total Time: 2 hrs 42 mins

Servings per Recipe: 6

Calories	456 kcal
Fat	23.5 g
Carbohydrates	43.9 g
Protein	20.9 g
Cholesterol	39 mg
Sodium	518 mg

Ingredients

1 lb. bison flank steak
1 1/2 tsp fajita seasoning
2 tbsp vegetable oil
2 cloves garlic, minced
1 fresh jalapeno pepper, seeded and chopped
1 large onion, thinly sliced
1 large green bell pepper, thinly sliced
1 large red or yellow bell pepper, thinly sliced
6 (8 inch) flour tortillas, warmed
Salsa
Sour cream
Lime wedges

Guacamole Salad:
2 Roma tomatoes, seeded and chopped
3 tbsp sliced green onions
1 fresh jalapeno pepper, seeded and chopped
2 cloves garlic, minced
1/2 tsp salt
1/4 tsp black pepper
2 large ripe avocados, halved, seeded, peeled, and coarsely mashed
Shredded romaine lettuce

Directions

1. Thinly slice the bison flank steak across the grain into bite-size strips and sprinkle with 1 tsp of the fajita seasoning.
2. Cover and chill for about 30 minutes.
3. In a large skillet, heat 1 tbsp of the oil on medium-high heat and sauté the garlic and the 1 jalapeño pepper for about 2 minutes.
4. Add the onion and sauté for about 6-8 minutes.
5. Transfer the onion mixture into a medium bowl.
6. Cover and keep warm.
7. In the same skillet, add the bell peppers and remaining 1/2 tsp of the fajita seasoning and cook for about 6-8 minutes.

8. Transfer the peppers into the bowl with onion mixture.
9. Cover and keep warm.
10. In the same skillet, heat the remaining 1 tbsp of the oil and cook 1/2 of the bison flank steak strips for about 1-2 minutes.
11. Transfer the strips into a bowl.
12. In the same skillet, cook the remaining bison flank steak strips.
13. Serve the bison flank steak and vegetables in the tortillas topped with salsa and sour cream.
14. Serve with the lime wedges and Guacamole Salad
15. For guacamole salad in a bowl, mix together the tomatoes, green onions, 1 jalapeño pepper, 2 cloves garlic, salt, and pepper.
16. Gently stir in the avocado and serve over the shredded romaine.

WESTERN PACIFIC
Fried Rice

Prep Time: 30 mins
Total Time: 50 mins

Servings per Recipe: 6
Calories	523 kcal
Fat	34.6 g
Carbohydrates	37.9g
Protein	14 g
Cholesterol	51 mg
Sodium	1253 mg

Ingredients

1 lb. bacon, chopped
4 cloves garlic, minced
6 green onions, chopped
2 carrots, sliced
1/2 lb. snow peas

4 C. cooked white rice
1/4 C. soy sauce

Directions

1. Heat a large skillet on medium-high heat and cook the bacon till browned completely.
2. Stir in the garlic, green onions and carrots and cook for about 2 minutes.
3. Stir in the snow peas and cook for about 2 minutes.
4. Stir in the cooked rice, 1 C. at a time, coating well with the grease.
5. Cook till the rice is heated completely.
6. Serve with a drizzling of the soy sauce.

Jade
Garden House Fried Rice

Prep Time: 10 mins
Total Time: 40 mins

Servings per Recipe: 8	
Calories	236 kcal
Fat	8.4 g
Carbohydrates	26.4g
Protein	13 g
Cholesterol	59 mg
Sodium	603 mg

Ingredients

1 1/2 C. uncooked white rice
3 tbsp sesame oil
1 small onion, chopped
1 clove garlic, chopped
1 C. small shrimp - peeled and deveined
1/2 C. diced ham
1 C. chopped cooked chicken breast
2 stalks celery, chopped
2 carrots - peeled and diced

1 green bell pepper, chopped
1/2 C. green peas
1 egg, beaten
1/4 C. soy sauce

Directions

1. Cook the rice according to package's directions.
2. Meanwhile in a large skillet. heat the sesame oil on medium-high heat and sauté the onion till golden.
3. Add the garlic and sauté till lightly browned.
4. Stir in the shrimp, ham and chicken and stir fry till the shrimp is pink.
5. Reduce the heat to medium,
6. Stir in the celery, carrot, green pepper and peas and stir fry till the vegetables become crisp-tender.
7. Stir in the beaten egg and cook till just scrambled.
8. Stir in the cooked rice and soy sauce and serve immediately.

FRIED RICE
Cauliflower

Prep Time: 15 mins
Total Time: 45 mins

Servings per Recipe: 6
Calories	366 kcal
Fat	19.2 g
Carbohydrates	15.8g
Protein	33.3 g
Cholesterol	132 mg
Sodium	1065 mg

Ingredients

2 C. frozen peas
1/2 C. water
1/4 C. sesame oil, divided
4 C. cubed pork loin
6 green onions, sliced
1 large carrot, cubed
2 cloves garlic, minced

20 oz. shredded cauliflower
6 tbsp soy sauce
2 eggs, beaten

Directions

1. In a pan, add the peas and water and bring to a boil.
2. Reduce the heat to medium-low and cook for about 5 minutes.
3. Drain the peas completely.
4. In a wok, heat 2 tbsp of the sesame oil on medium-high heat and sear the pork for about 7-10 minutes.
5. Transfer the pork into a plate.
6. In the same wok, heat the remaining 2 tbsp of the sesame oil and sauté the green onions, carrot and garlic for about 5 minutes.
7. Stir in the cauliflower and cook for about 4-5 minutes.
8. Stir in the pork, peas and and soy sauce and stir fry for about 3-5 minutes.
9. Push the pork mixture to one side of the wok.
10. Add the beaten eggs and cook for about 3-5 minutes, stirring continuously.
11. Stir the cooked eggs into the pork mixture, breaking up any large chunks.
12. Serve hot.

Printed in Great Britain
by Amazon

84474402R00063